RE-DISCOVERING
Britain
1750–1900

Titles in this series:

Acknowledgements

Photographs reproduced by kind permission of:

Cover 'Death or Liberty!' or Britannia and the Virtues of the Constitution in Danger of Violation from the Great Political Libertine, Radical Reform' pub. by H. Humphrey 1819 (coloured etching) by George Cruikshank (1792–1878) Private Collection/ Bridgeman Art Library; **p.v** *from top* Mary Evans Picture Library; To Brighton and Back for Three and Sixpence, 1859 (oil and canvas) by Charles Rossiter (1827–97) Birmingham Museums and Art Gallery/ Bridgeman Art Library; The Fotomas Index; Ford Madox Brown *Work* © Manchester City Art Galleries; **p.vi** *l* Mary Evans Picture Library; *m* Trustees of the Wedgwood Museum, Barlaston, Staffordshire; *r* Hulton Archives; **p.1** *l* 'Death or Liberty!' or Britannia and the Virtues of the Constitution in Danger of Violation from the Great Political Libertine, Radical Reform', pub, by H. Humphrey, 1819 (coloured etching) by George Cruikshank (1792–1878) Private Collection/Bridgeman Art Library; *m* Mary Evans Picture Library; *r* The London Borough of Hackney Archives Department; **p.4** Cottage Industry, 1791 (engraving) by William Hincks (1752–97) (after) British Library, London, UK/Bridgeman Art Library; **p.5** © Tate, London; **pp.6, 7** Hulton Archives **p.8** Mary Evans Picture Library; **p.9** Hulton Archives; **p.10** *tr* Mansell Collection/Time Pix; *ml* Mansell Collection/Time Pix; *mr* Mary Evans Picture Library; *br* Ford Madox Brown *Work* © Manchester City Art Galleries; **p.11** Industry of the Tyne: Iron and Coal, 1801 (oil on canvas) by William Bell Scott (1811–90) Wallington Hall, Northumberland, UK/Bridgeman Art Library; **p.14** Trustees of the Wedgwood Museum, Barlaston, Staffordshire; **p.15** *t* Trustees of the Wedgwood Museum, Barlaston, Staffordshire; *b* Josiah Wedgwood (1730–95), engraved and pub. by George Townley Stubbs (1756–1815), 1795 (stipple engraving) by George Stubbs (1724–1806) (after) Private Collection/Bridgeman Art Library; **p.16** Mary Evans Picture Library; **p.19** The Arkwright Society; **p.20** Sir Richard Arkwright (1732–92), inventor of the Spinning Jenny by Joseph Wright of Derby (1734–97) Philip Mould, Historical Portraits Ltd, London, UK/Bridgeman Art Library; **p.24** *t* The Arkwright Society; *b* Mary Evans Picture Library; **p.26** Hulton Archives; **pp.27, 30, 31, 33** Mary Evans Picture Library; **p.35** The Art Archive/Eileen Tweedy; **p.36–37** Courtesy of the Museum of London; **p.42** *both* Fotomas Index; **pp.44, 45** Mansell Collection/Time Pix; **p.46** *t* Wilberforce House: Kingston Upon Hull City Museums and Art Galleries; *b* Mansell Collection/Time Pix; **p.47** Slaves Fell the Ripe Sugar, Antigua, 1823 (print) by W. Clark (fl.1823) British Library, London, UK/Bridgeman Art Library; **p.48** *both* Fotomas Index; **p.49** Mansell Collection/Time Pix; **p.51** Trustees of the Wedgwood Museum, Barlaston, Staffordshire; **p.52** Portrait of a Negro Man, Olaudah Equiano, 1780s (previously attributed to Joshua Reynolds) by English School (18th century) Royal Albert Memorial Museum Exeter, Devon, UK/Bridgeman Art Library; **p.53** Mary Evans Picture Library; **p.54** By courtesy of the National Portrait Gallery, London; **p.57** Mary Evans Picture Library; **p.59** Private Collection/ Photograph by National Portrait Gallery, London; **p.60** The Art Archive/Eileen Tweedy; **pp.61, 63** Mary Evans Picture Library; **p.64** Mansell Collection/Time Pix; **p.65** Mary Evans Picture Library; **p.72** *both* Hulton Archives; **p.73** Hulton Archives; **p.74** *t* Hulton Archives; *b* Mary Evans Picture Library; **p.75** *both* Brighton Local Studies Library; **p.76** *t* © Punch Library; *b* Hulton Archives; **p.77** To Brighton and Back for Three and Sixpence, 1859 (oil and canvas) by Charles Rossiter (1827–97) Birmingham Museums and Art Gallery/ Bridgeman Art Library; **p.78** St Pancras Hotel and Station from Pentonville Road by John O'Connor (1830–89) Museum of London, UK/Bridgeman Art Library; **p.79** *t* Hulton Archives; *b* The Art Archive/Eileen Tweedy; **p.80** *t* Mary Evans Picture Library; **pp.81, 85** Mary Evans Picture Library; **p.90** 'Death or Liberty!' or Britannia and the Virtues of the Constitution in Danger of Violation from the Great Political Libertine, Radical Reform', pub. by H. Humphrey, 1819 (coloured etching) by George Cruikshank (1792–1878) Private Collection/Bridgeman Art Library; **p.91** Fotomas Index; **p.92** Mary Evans Picture Library; **p.95** *t* Hulton Archives; *b* Mansell Collection/ Time Pix; **p.96** *tl* Mary Evans Picture Library; *tr* By permission of the British Library; *bl* By permission of the National Museum of Labour History; **p.97** Mary Evans Picture Library; **p.99** Ford Madox Brown *Work* © Manchester City Art Galleries; **p.101** *b* © Tate, London; **p.102** Many Happy Returns of the Day by William Powell Frith (1819–1909) Harrogate Museums and Art Gallery, North Yorkshire, UK/Bridgeman Art Library; **p.103** Cromer Museum, Norfolk Museums and Archaeological Service; **p.104** *t* The Art Archive/ Eileen Tweedy *b* Mansell Collection/Time Pix; **p.105** Triumph of Steam and Electricity from 'The Illustrated London News' 1897, Guildhall Library Corporation of London, UK/Bridgeman Art Library; **p.107** *b* Mansell Collection/Time Pix; **p.110** Hulton Archives; **p.111** *t* Mansell Collection/Time Pix; *b* The London Borough of Hackney Archives Department.

t = top, *m* = middle, *b* = bottom, *l* = left, *r* = right

Written text reproduced by kind permission of:

p.62 Terry Deary, *The Vile Victorians*, Scholastic Ltd 'Horrible Histories', 1994

Every effort has been made to trace all copyright holders, but if any have been inadvertently overlooked the publishers will be pleased to make the necessary arrangements at the first opportunity.

THE SCHOOLS HISTORY PROJECT
S·H·P
OFFICIAL TEXT

RE-DISCOVERING
Britain
1750–1900

Colin Shephard
Andy Reid
Series Editor:
Colin Shephard
Consultant Editor:
Dave Martin

JOHN MURRAY

The Schools History Project

The Project was set up in 1972, with the aim of improving the study of history for students aged 13–16. This involved a reconsideration of the ways in which history contributes to the educational needs of young people. The Project devised new objectives, new criteria for planning and developing courses, and the materials to support them. New examinations, requiring new methods of assessment, also had to be developed. These have continued to be popular. The advent of GCSE in 1987 led to the expansion of Project approaches into other syllabuses.

The Schools History Project has been based at Trinity and All Saints College, Leeds, since 1978, from where it supports teachers through a biennial Bulletin, regular INSET, an annual Conference and a website (www.tasc.ac.uk/shp).

Since the National Curriculum was drawn up in 1991, the Project has continued to expand its publications, bringing its ideas to courses for Key Stage 3 as well as a range of GCSE and A level specifications.

Words printed in SMALL CAPITALS are defined in the Glossary on page 113.

Note: The wording and sentence structure of some written sources have been adapted and simplified to make them accessible to all pupils, while faithfully preserving the sense of the original.

© Colin Shephard, Andy Reid 1993 with revisions by Dave Martin 2001

First published in 1993 as part of *Peace and War* by
John Murray (Publishers) Ltd, a member of the Hodder Headline Group
338 Euston Road,
London NW1 3BH

This completely revised edition first published 2001

Reprinted 2002, 2003, 2004

Layouts by Alison Bond/Bondi Design
Artwork by Countryside Illustrations, Jon Davis/Linden Artists, Patricia Ludlow/Linden Artists, Tony Randell and Steve Smith.
Colour separations by Colourscript, Mildenhall, Suffolk
Typeset in 11½/13pt Concorde by Wearset, Boldon, Tyne and Wear
Printed and bound in Great Britain by Butler & Tanner, Frome and London

A catalogue entry for this title is available from the British Library

ISBN 0 7195 8546 5
Teachers' Resource Book ISBN 0 7195 8547 3

Contents

1771 Arkwright opens his first factory

1807 The slave trade is abolished in Britain

1830 The first 'inter-city' railway is opened

1750   **1775**   **1800**   **1825**

The eighteenth century

The nineteenth century

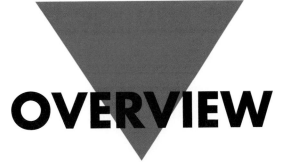

OVERVIEW

HOW DID BRITAIN CHANGE BETWEEN 1750 AND 1900?

1832 The Great Reform Act

1857 Indian soldiers rebel against British rule

1888 Match girls' strike

1850   1875   1900

The Victorian period (when Victoria was Queen)

How did Britain change between 1750 and 1900?

▶▶ In this book you are going to find out about life in Britain between 1750 and 1900. Pages 2–9 give you an overview of the main changes from 1750 to 1825 to 1900.

1750

▼ **ACTIVITY**

1 **Work with a partner. Look at these two pictures and list all the changes you can see between 1750 and 1900.**

2 **Would you say there was**
   a) a lot of change   b) not much change
   between 1750 and 1900?
   Write a paragraph to explain your answer.

By the end of this book you should be able to explain these changes in a lot more detail.

1900

▶▶ **Pages 2–3 showed you some of the changes which are easy to see. Over the next six pages you will look at some of these changes in more detail. You will also find out about some changes which are harder to see.**

1750

▼ ACTIVITY

You are going to describe and explain how Britain changed between 1750 and 1900.

1 **Work in groups of six. Choose one of the following topics: Population, Work, Health and medicine, Travel, Education or The Vote.**
2 **Make three cards for your topic headed 1750, 1825 and 1900.**
3 **As you work through pages 4–9 make notes about your topic on the card for each period.**

Population

■ Total population about 11 million:

England	Ireland	Scotland	Wales
5.8 m	3.2 m	1.2 m	0.5 m

■ About 80 per cent of people lived and worked in the countryside.
■ Many babies died before their first birthday.
■ The annual death rate was 28 deaths per 1000 people.

Work

■ The most important work was in farming – food and wool production in particular.
■ All industries were small-scale. Manufacturing was done in people's homes, or in workshops attached to their homes.
■ The power to make machines work was provided by waterwheels, or by horses, or by human hands or feet.
■ Steam power was used to pump water from some mines.

▼ SOURCE 1 *Major cities and industries in 1750*

Key
○ Towns over 100,000 population
⚒ Iron
🛒 Coal
⚙ Cotton and silk
⛏ Metal mining

N

0   100 km

▲ SOURCE 2 *Spinning flax at home, an engraving from 1791. The woman on the right is reeling the spun thread ready to hand it on to the weavers, who will weave it into cloth*

▲ **SOURCE 3** *A nineteenth-century painting of an English 'dame school' in the eighteenth century. Children were often sent here to be minded while their parents worked, rather than for an education*

Education
- Most children in England and Wales did not go to school at all and few could read or write.
- In Scotland all parishes had schools and most people could read and write.
- There were two universities in England, four in Scotland and one in Ireland.

Health and medicine
- People did not know that germs caused disease and could do little to fight diseases like smallpox and diphtheria, which killed many people.
- Only simple operations on patients were possible, because there were no anaesthetics. Patients often died from shock or infection.

The vote
- Only five per cent of the population could vote in elections for the House of Commons.
- No women were allowed to vote.

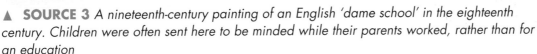

Travel
It took ten to twelve days to travel from London to Edinburgh by road.

Population

- Total population about 20 million:
  England
  11.4 m
  Ireland
  6.8 m
  Scotland
  1.6 m
  Wales
  0.6 m
- About 60 per cent of people lived and worked in the countryside.
- Many babies still died in their first year of life, but families were very large.
- The annual death rate was 22 deaths per 1000 people.

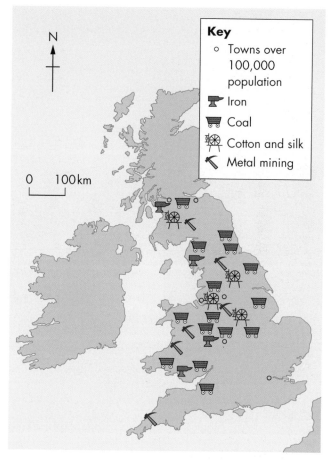

▲ **SOURCE 4** *Major cities and industries in 1825*

Work

- Farmers were growing more food than in 1750.
- The cotton industry was now bigger and more important than the wool industry.
- Many people still worked in small workshops, but some industries were now based in factories.
- Since 1750 coal production had tripled, and iron production had increased by ten times.
- Steam power was used to drive machines in factories.

▶ **SOURCE 5** *Children working in the winding room of a cotton mill in 1820*

Education

- Most middle-class and upper-class boys (but not many girls) went to school.
- Elementary schools in England and Wales provided education for the children of the poor if they wanted to attend. Many did not because they had to work instead.
- No new universities had been set up since 1750.

Health and medicine

- A vaccine had been developed for smallpox, but there were no other vaccines because people still did not know that germs caused disease.
- So many people were crowded into towns like Leeds that killer diseases such as cholera, typhoid and tuberculosis spread rapidly because of infected water, dirty living conditions and poor diet.
- Only simple operations were possible because there were no anaesthetics. Patients often died from shock or infection.

The vote

- Five per cent of the population could vote in elections for the House of Commons.
- No women were allowed to vote.
- Most of Britain's new and growing cities were not allowed to elect their own MPs.
- Demands for 'parliamentary reform' were made at large meetings.

▲ **SOURCE 6** *A 'ragged school' in London in the mid-nineteenth century. Ragged schools for the poor were set up by charities in some areas*

Travel

It now took only 45 hours to travel from London to Edinburgh by road.

Population

- Total population about 42 million:

    England
    30.5 m

    Ireland
    4.5 m

    Scotland
    4.5 m

    Wales
    2 m

- The population of England had risen at a rapid rate since 1825. In Scotland and Wales the population was also rising, but more slowly than in England. The population of Ireland had actually fallen, owing to a dreadful famine and the emigration that followed it.

- About 30 per cent of people lived and worked in the countryside. Many large towns and cities had developed.

- The annual death rate was 18 deaths per 1000 people.

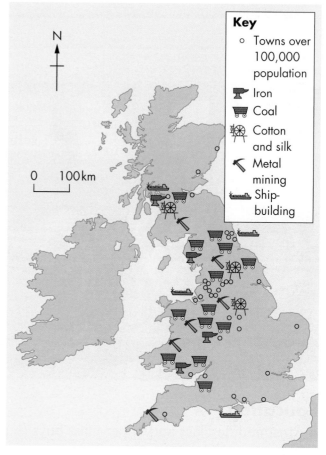

▲ **SOURCE 7** *Major cities and industries in 1900*

▼ **SOURCE 8** *Inside a Lancashire cotton mill*

Work

- The most important industries were coal, iron, steel and textiles (mostly cotton cloth).
- Most industry was now based in factories.
- Many farmers now used machines, although the machines were still mostly horse powered.
- Steam power had been introduced into most industries, even in small factories and workshops.

Education

- School was compulsory for all five- to twelve-year-olds, both boys and girls.
- Many more people could read and write.
- There were ten universities in England, five in Scotland, one in Ireland and one in Wales.

▼ **SOURCE 9** *A local council school in 1908*

Health and medicine

- Louis Pasteur had discovered that germs cause diseases. This led to vaccines being developed for diphtheria and other diseases.
- Anaesthetics and antiseptics were developed. Most patients no longer died from shock or infection.
- Local councils began to improve water supplies and sewers to improve the health of people in towns.

The vote

- Most men could now vote, but women could not.
- Parliament included many MPs from the growing industrial towns and fewer from country areas.

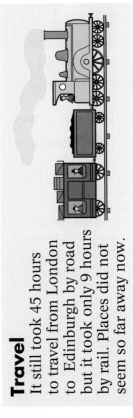

Travel
It still took 45 hours to travel from London to Edinburgh by road but it took only 9 hours by rail. Places did not seem so far away now.

▼ **ACTIVITY**

You should each have completed three cards for your chosen topic.

1 Compare what you have written on your cards. Look for changes between the three dates.
2 Now, on the 1825 card, write two or three sentences to explain how Britain changed between 1750 and 1825.
3 On the 1900 card write two or three sentences to explain how Britain changed between 1825 and 1900.

▼ **DISCUSS**

In your group, each person report their findings, then discuss the following questions.

4 In which topic was there greatest change between 1750 and 1825?
5 In which topic was there greatest change between 1825 and 1900?
6 As a result of these changes did life get better or worse for the people of Britain?

Your pathway

In the rest of this book you will be studying these changes in greater depth.

Depth Study 1: The Industrial Revolution
You will compare the lives of two successful businessmen: Josiah Wedgwood and Richard Arkwright. You will also look at what life was like for children who worked in the factories.

Depth Study 2: Empire and trade
You will find out about the growth of Britain's trade and Empire. You will find out:

- why the slave trade was so successful yet so cruel and why it was abolished
- about the thread joining Britain and India

and you will decide who benefited most from the British Empire.

Depth Study 3: Towns
You will investigate what it was like to live in a town. You will try to answer the question, 'If towns and cities were so awful, why did so many people choose to live in them?'

Depth Study 4: The vote
You will find out about people's attempts to gain the right to vote and you will consider whether or not the Chartists were revolutionaries.

Depth Study 5: The Victorians
You will find out what people thought was important in the nineteenth century.

DEPTH STUDY 1

THE INDUSTRIAL REVOLUTION

Beautiful industry!
In a northern town a smartly dressed young child is sitting quietly beside a raging coal furnace. Powerful labourers hammer on regardless.

It's an unlikely scene. The heat would have been unbearable and the sound deafening, but this painter did not set out to be realistic. He wanted to get across a simple message. His message was that industry was here to stay and it was a **good thing**.

In this depth study you will find out how some people agreed with the artist that industry was good, while others were less sure. But industry is a vast topic. So you are going to focus mainly on one industry – the cotton industry.

Why was British industry so successful?

Between 1750 and 1900 Britain's industry led the world. On these two pages you will discover some reasons why it was so successful.

In history there is rarely a simple answer to the question 'why?' Any big changes usually happen because of a combination of factors. The people on pages 12–13 are describing different factors that were important.

▼ ACTIVITY

Write each of the following headings on a separate card.

- **More food**
- **Plenty of** RAW MATERIALS
- **Growing population**
- **Growing overseas trade**
- **Better transport**
- **Talented individuals**

Write one or more sentences to summarise why each factor helped industry to succeed.
   Keep your cards. They will help you to understand how men like Josiah Wedgwood (pages 14–15) and Richard Arkwright (pages 16–21) did so well.

Because . . . the population was growing quickly

> The more people there are, the more goods we buy.

> The more children we have the more workers there are for the new industries.

Because . . . Britain had plenty of raw materials

> We have plenty of iron to make machines, railways and cannons.

> We have plenty of coal to drive steam engines in the factories.

> We have plenty of clay to supply the pottery industry.

Because . . . Britain's farmers grew more food

We produce more food for the growing population, particularly for people in towns who can not grow their own food.

We farm workers earn more and so we have more money to spend on goods produced by industry.

Because . . . Britain's Empire and overseas trade were growing

We traders make money, and INVEST it in improving British industry and transport.

We buy lots of British goods, e.g. cotton cloth. This keeps the factories and workers busy back in Britain.

We bring in raw materials like cotton from America.

Because . . . Britain's transport was improved

Better transport makes raw materials cheaper, and makes the supply more reliable.

Better transport enlarges the MARKETS and makes the finished goods cheaper.

Better transport allows new ideas and inventions to spread more quickly.

Because . . . Britain had talented entrepreneurs and inventors

Britain has great inventors who have ideas about how to improve industry.

Then it's us ENTREPRENEURS who can see how to make money out of these new ideas and inventions.

Case study 1: What made Josiah Wedgwood successful?

▶▶ **Josiah Wedgwood was a successful pottery maker. This story strip tells you about his career. What were the secrets of his success?**

▼ DISCUSS

1 Study the story of Wedgwood's career. Discuss what the 'secrets of his success' were.
2 Which of the factors described on pages 12–13 affected the development of his pottery business?
3 Explain *how* each one helped him succeed.
4 Which factor do you think was the most important in helping him succeed? Give reasons.

1 Josiah Wedgwood started work as a potter in the family business at the age of nine after his father died.

My pottery could be as good as this stuff.

5 All the finest pottery, the kind that the rich wanted, was still imported from other countries. Wedgwood thought that he could compete with that.

4 He produced good pottery at low prices. Poor people flocked to buy it.

8 At the age of 38 the problems with his right leg became so bad that it had to be AMPUTATED. Surprisingly he survived the operation and got about on a wooden artificial leg.

9 As a successful businessman he now had enough money to invest in building a canal to improve transport.

12 He invested his profits in a grand house called Etruria Hall for his family and in good housing for his workers. He also found the time to be a founder member of the Society for the ABOLITION of the Slave Trade.

13 He knew the value of good publicity. He had a showroom in London, published a catalogue and employed salesmen to sell his china at home and overseas.

2 After an attack of smallpox at the age of twelve his health was damaged. He had a permanent problem with his right leg. Unable to work, he studied the craft of pottery

3 He saved £20 and set up his own business in Staffordshire, aged 28. He hired the best workers and worked them hard.

6 He was a great experimenter and inventor. He invented new machines and new glazes which he kept secret from his rivals.

7 He produced high-quality fine china. After selling a tea service to Queen Charlotte he was able to call himself 'Potter to Her Majesty'.

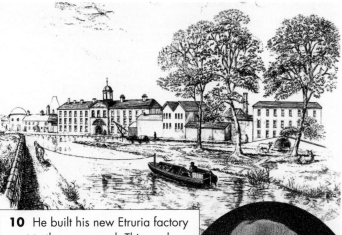

10 He built his new Etruria factory next to the new canal. This made it cheaper and easier to bring in clay from Cornwall and Devon and coal to fuel his kilns, and to transport his fragile pottery to market.

11 In his new, bigger factory he could employ more people. He developed the system of the DIVISION OF LABOUR. He employed famous artists to decorate pots and continued to experiment with new ideas.

14 His greatest success was selling a 952-piece dinner service to the Russian Empress Catherine the Great. He was the most famous potter in Europe.

◄ **SOURCE 1**
Josiah Wedgwood (1730–1795), painted in 1795 by George Stubbs

Case study 2: What made Richard Arkwright successful?

▶▶ **Richard Arkwright made a fortune out of the cotton industry and his factories helped change the way people worked. Pages 16–21 tell you about his career.**

Steps to success: the Richard Arkwright story

Richard Arkwright was born in 1732, the thirteenth and youngest child of a tailor. He was apprenticed to a barber but was very ambitious. By the age of thirty he had started his own wig-making business and he travelled around the country collecting hair.

Here are seven steps to his success:

Step 1: Speed up spinning
Coming from a tailor's family, Arkwright knew a lot about the cloth industry. In 1733 an invention called a 'flying shuttle' had speeded up weaving. Lots of raw cotton was being imported, to be made into cloth, but spinners could not work quickly enough now to supply the weavers with thread. Arkwright employed John Kay and some craftsmen to develop a machine, a 'spinning frame', to produce cotton thread more quickly. Others had tried this but had not been very successful.

Step 2: Get a patent
Arkwright saw the potential to make money and he went into partnership with four businessmen. He used his partners' money to take out a PATENT. He set up his 'spinning frame' in a factory in Nottingham. The frame was powered by horses walking round and round in a circle.

▲ **SOURCE 1** *Sir Richard Arkwright*

Step 3: Build a factory
The 'spinning frame' could also be powered by a water wheel. In 1771, Arkwright and his partners built a cotton-spinning mill at Cromford in Derbyshire. The water wheel was turned by a fast-flowing stream which had been cut to drain the local lead mines. The water from the mines was slightly warm so it never froze in winter. The 'spinning frame' now became known as the 'water frame'.

▶ **SOURCE 2** *Illustration of the first Cromford mill from the Mirror magazine, 1836*

Step 4: Find some workers

Arkwright needed a lot of workers but in Cromford there were not enough people. He built a large number of cottages close to the factory and then advertised for workers to come to Cromford. He preferred weavers with large families as children could do much of the work. Two-thirds of his employees were children. Unlike some employers he would not employ children under the age of six years.

Step 5: Expand your business

The water frame was very successful and Arkwright planned more factories. His one remaining partner thought that this was too risky, so Arkwright carried on alone. He built successful factories in England and Scotland.

Step 6: Defend your invention

Many MANUFACTURERS in Britain and abroad copied his ideas. Arkwright tried to make these people pay to use his invention and he became very unpopular. His patents were also challenged. Some people claimed that he had 'borrowed' his ideas from other inventors. This did not stop his success.

Step 7: Enjoy your wealth

Arkwright became very rich and bought a country estate. He built himself a large mansion and then later a castle to live in. When he died in 1792 he was worth about half a million pounds, a huge sum at that time.

▼ DISCUSS

1 Study Richard Arkwright's story.
2 How did each of his 'Steps to success' help his business to succeed?
3 Which 'step' was most important in helping him succeed?
4 Compare Richard Arkwright to Josiah Wedgwood. How are their lives and business careers similar and how are they different?

▼ ACTIVITY

1 Now that you have found out about Richard Arkwright, draw or describe a story strip of his life. You could model it on the one for Josiah Wedgwood on pages 14–15. You could start like this:

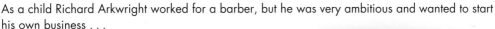

As a child Richard Arkwright worked for a barber, but he was very ambitious and wanted to start his own business . . .

You should then include at least one frame for each 'step' in his story.

2 Leave space for a final frame which explains

■ why and how he changed the cotton industry
■ what impact he had on the lives of people at the time.

You will be able to complete this frame when you have studied the next four pages.

How did Arkwright's mills change the way people worked?

In the DOMESTIC SYSTEM most workers worked at home, as in Source 3. At Cromford they worked in specially built factories, usually called mills. Let's look at the differences.

▲ **SOURCE 3** *Inside a cotton worker's cottage in 1750. Spinning was usually done by women. The spinning wheel turned cotton or wool into thread. The wheel was turned by hand or foot power. It was fairly skilled work. Spinners worked long hours but decided for themselves when they did it. At certain times of year they would also do other work such as farming. The cotton was then woven into cloth. This was usually done upstairs where the larger windows gave more light*

▼ **SOURCE 4**
Arkwright's water frame produced better cotton thread more quickly than any other method. 128 bobbins of thread could be produced at the same time by each machine. The frame was so large that it needed a lot of space to set it up and so heavy that it could not be worked by hand. It was turned by water power. It was so simple that a child could operate it. The mills never stopped working. They kept going 24 hours a day. The workers worked in shifts of often more than 12 hours per day, all year round

▼ **ACTIVITY**

Draw up a list of differences between the methods of spinning used before Arkwright's machine and mills, and the methods used after these developments. Find as many as you can. Think about who **did the spinning,** where **they did it,** when **they did it and** how **they did it.**

People reacted in different ways to these new mills. To some they were beautiful, while others, like William Blake, called them 'dark Satanic mills'.

Grace cottage

Counting house

Warehouse

Bow fronted house

First mill

Third mill

Warehouse

Second mill

Factory manager's house

▲ **SOURCE 5** *A photograph of the Cromford mills today*

▼ **DISCUSS**

The Cromford mills are preserved by the Arkwright Society. More than 100,000 people visit the site each year. It is possible that these and other mills in the River Derwent valley may become a 'World Heritage Site', like other important places such as Stonehenge and the Taj Mahal in India.

1 **Do you think it is important to preserve the Cromford mills? Give reasons.**
2 **If you think it is important, then who should pay?**

What did people think of Arkwright?

▼ **SOURCE 6** *Written by Josiah Wedgwood in a letter to James Watt, another successful businessman, in 1785. Wedgwood met Arkwright several times and sold him a 'Queen's ware' dinner service*

Mr Arkwright . . . invites me to come and see him as often as I can, although he tells me he at present avoids all company because it robs him of his time and breaks in upon his plans. And besides, he is no company for people who visit him, for whilst they are talking to him upon one subject he is thinking upon another, and does not know what they say to him.

▼ **SOURCE 7** *Written by a painter, Joseph Farington, in his diary in 1801 about child workers at Richard Arkwright's mills at Cromford*

In the evening I walked to Cromford, and saw the children coming from their work . . . I was glad to see them look in general very healthy, many with fine, rosy complexions.

These children had been at work from six or seven o'clock this morning and it was now near seven in the evening. The time for resting allowed them is at twelve o'clock 40 minutes, during which time they dine.

One boy of ten or eleven years of age told me his wages were 3s 6d a week – and a little girl told me her wages were 2s 3d a week.

These children are employed in Mr Arkwright's works in the week days, and on Sundays attend a school where they receive education. They came to chapel in regular order and looked healthy and well and were decently clothed and clean . . .

1732 Arkwright's birth

1700 1750 1785 1781 1800 1801 1835 1850

1792 Arkwright died

▼ **SOURCE 8** *Adapted from the diary of Sylas Neville, an eighteenth-century traveller, written in 1781*

Arkwright appears to be a man of great understanding. He knows how to make people do their best. He not only rewards them, but gives special clothes to the most successful workers, which makes others want to copy them.

He also gives two parties at the Greyhound [a hotel in Cromford, built by Arkwright] to the workmen and their wives and families with a week's holiday at the time of each party. This makes them hardworking and sober all the rest of the year.

▼ **SOURCE 9** *Written by Matthew Boulton, a successful businessman, in a letter to his partner, James Watt, in 1781*

Arkwright swears that he will ruin those Manchester rascals [who had used his invention without his permission]. It is agreed by all who know him that he is a Tyrant.

▲ **SOURCE 10**

Sir Richard Arkwright (1732–1792) painted at Arkwright's request by Joseph Wright of Derby c. 1790

▼ **SOURCE 11** *Written by the historian Edward Baines in his* History of Cotton Manufacture in Great Britain, *published in 1835*

That he might not waste a moment Arkwright generally travelled with four horses, and at a very rapid speed.

His businesses in Derbyshire, Lancashire and Scotland were so many and widespread that they showed his astonishing power of doing business and his all-grasping spirit.

In many of these businesses he had partners, but he generally managed in such a way that whoever lost, he himself was a gainer.

So unbounded was his confidence in the success of his machinery, and in the wealth to be produced by it, that he would say that he would pay off the government's debt.

1900　　1950　1968　2000

▼ **SOURCE 12** *Written by a historian, E.J. Hobsbawm, in* Industry and Empire, *published in 1968*

The water frame was not the original idea of Richard Arkwright (although he patented it). Arkwright was an unscrupulous operator who – unlike most real inventors of the period – became very rich.

▼ **DISCUSS**

Study the sources on these two pages.

1 Which aspects of Arkwright's character were important to his success as a businessman?
2 Which of these aspects do you think was the most important?
3 Look closely at the dates of the sources. Arkwright died in 1792. When were Arkwright and his achievements (a) most admired and (b) most criticised? Was it:

■ in his lifetime
■ in the nineteenth century
■ in the twentieth century?

4 Why do you think people's views on Arkwright changed?
5 'Richard Arkwright invented factories and so changed the course of history.' Do you agree or disagree with this statement? Give reasons.

▼ **ACTIVITY**

Now that you know about the way Arkwright changed the cotton industry, go back to your story strip from page 17 and complete the final frame.

Children in the mills

The most common criticism of the textile mills was that child workers were mistreated. On pages 22–29 you will find out what the critics were worried about. You will use your findings to help you write a story about children in the mills.

Tom's story

Tom's heart was racing. Bryson was coming towards him, strap in hand. He was in for a beating. He knew it. But suddenly, a terrifying noise much louder than the machines hit his ears and Bryson stopped in his tracks. It was a grinding noise. It sounded like a monster dying, and as it died it ground its teeth together. There was another noise, too. This one sounded like a whistle. But it was not a whistle. It was a person screaming. It soon stopped.

Bryson raced towards the noise. Some workers were holding their hands over their faces. They were too scared to look at the horrible sight. Two men were trying to stop the machine. Whirling around the giant shaft was something that looked like a bundle of red rags. Each time the bundle reached the driving wheel of the machine, it was forced through the small gap. This made the engine moan and grind like an animal in pain.

A crowd of workers had gathered. They had seen what had happened. The bundle was not rags at all. It was Ellen. None of the machines had guards on, and the string from her apron had got stuck in the shaft. It had wound round like a fishing reel and pulled her in. It was almost as if the machine had taken her for food.

▼ DISCUSS

1 The writer of Tom's story has been very clever in getting us interested. How has she done that?
2 Do you think the incident she describes actually happened? Explain your answer.

▼ STORY WRITING

Tom's story is a piece of historical fiction set in a nineteenth-century cotton mill. Quite a lot of what ordinary people know about the past comes from historical fiction like this, in novels or on television and film. Some of it is quite well researched and accurate. Some is not.

You are now going to try to write your own well-researched story.

3 You are going to study the evidence on pages 24–29 and then write your own short story about children in the mills.

For your short story you must follow this story recipe:

■ The year is 1819.
■ The events of your story happen inside a cotton mill.
■ Your story covers all or part of a single day shift, between 5 a.m. and 8 p.m.
■ Your story may have no more than three main characters.

Remember that a good story is one that is interesting but believable. You need:

■ a setting that is authentic
■ characters that your reader cares about
■ a plot that your reader will find believable.

First make notes in a table like this. Make it big. There might be a lot to record.

	Historical notes	Story ideas
Setting (e.g. What kind of mill? Where? How big? What time of year? What time of day?)		
Characters		
Plot (e.g. What real-life incidents from pages 24–29 could you include?)		

Who were the child workers?

Many of the early mill owners employed large numbers of children. This was not new or shocking. In the domestic system children had worked at home.

Orphans

Some of the children in the mills were PAUPER APPRENTICES. They were orphans, who were sent to the mills by the authorities who looked after them in the large towns. The factory owner agreed to feed and clothe them. They lived in an 'apprentice house' near the mill. OVERSEERS were given the job of making the children work as hard as possible. The more work the children did, the more the overseers were paid.

Poor families

Other child workers were the sons and daughters of adult workers. One employer, David Dale (see Source 3), sent out advertisements to the Highland areas of Scotland where there was a lot of poverty and unemployment. He invited whole families to come and work for him.

Why did the mill owners want child workers?

Mill owners liked to have children as workers.

- Machines like the 'water frame' were automatic, so children were able to run them. They had only to make sure that threads did not snap during spinning.
- Children were paid less than adults, and apprentices were not paid at all.
- Children were also more agile, so it was easier for them to crawl under the machines to repair broken threads and to clean away dust or loose threads.

What did the children do?

You can see the range of jobs in Source 4.

Cotton Mill, Cromford, 10th Dec. 1771.

WANTED immediately, two Journeymen Clock-Makers, or others that underſtands Tooth and Pinion well: Alſo a Smith that can forge and file.—Likewiſe two Wood Turners that have been accuſtomed to Wheel-making, Spoke-turning, &c. Weavers reſiding in this Neighbourhood, by applying at the Mill, may have good Work. There is Employment at the above Place, for Women, Children, &c. and good Wages.

N. B. A Quantity of Box Wood is wanted: Any Perſons whom the above may ſuit, will be treated with by Meſſrs. Arkwright and Co. at the Mill, or Mr. Strutt, in Derby.

Derby Mercury 1771.

7

▲ **SOURCE 1** *An advertisement placed by Richard Arkwright in the Derby Mercury, December 1771*

▼ **SOURCE 2** *This picture, 'Carding, Drawing and Roving in a Cotton Mill', was originally an illustration for a book called* The History of Cotton Manufacture in Great Britain, *published in 1835. The author was Edward Baines, editor of a newspaper, the* Northern Mercury. *In his newspaper Baines often defended the mill owners and how they ran their cotton mills. This mill looks light and airy but in fact it would have been hot and humid, with the air full of cotton dust*

▼ **SOURCE 3** *A letter written in 1791 by a mill owner, David Dale*

I have information that there are persons crossing the islands to entice the poor people to go to America. I have therefore sent information to all places where people are proposing to leave their native country to advertise to them that they may have work here in the Lowlands, and I have pledged myself to build houses near the mill for 200 families.

▼ **SOURCE 4** *A modern artist's impression of a cotton mill in 1819. If you would like to know more about any of the activities and jobs in the factory you can get a sheet from your teacher to help you*

▼ **STORY WRITING**

1 **You should now be able to fill in some historical notes in the setting and character boxes in your table.**
2 **Record your story ideas if you have any.**

How were the child workers treated?

Some people became worried about these child workers. They started a campaign to ban child labour which quickly gathered momentum. Almost all of the sources from this period are biased one way or another. They were either created by supporters of the mill owners or by critics of child labour. So watch out for source warning stamps like this. Read those sources carefully.

SOURCE WARNING!

▼ **SOURCE 5** *An extract from the Memoir of Robert Blincoe. Robert Blincoe was an orphan who worked in the mills as an apprentice from the age of seven. He became so deformed because of the work that he left and worked for himself at home. He published his memoir, under the name of John Brown, in 1828. This extract describes his first day at work. Historians now agree that these stories were made up by Blincoe*

They reached the mill about half-past five [in the morning]. The moment he entered the doors, the noise appalled him, and the stench [smell] seemed intolerable.

The task first given him was to pick up the loose cotton that fell upon the floor. Apparently nothing could be easier and he set to eagerly, although much terrified by the whirling motion and noise of the machinery, and not a little affected by the dust and flue [fluff] with which he was half suffocated.

Unused to the stench he soon felt sick and, by constantly stooping, his back ached. He therefore sat down, but this he soon found was strictly forbidden. His taskmaster gave him to understand he must keep on his legs. He did so, till twelve o'clock. Blincoe suffered greatly with thirst and hunger.

▼ **SOURCE 6** *In 1833 Robert Blincoe was invited to give evidence to Parliament about conditions in the mills*

I have seen the time when two handles of a pound [0.5 kg] weight each have been screwed to my ears. Then three or four of us have been hung on a cross-beam above the machinery, hanging by our hands. Mind, we were apprentices without a father or mother to take care of us. Then we used to stand up, in a skip, without our shirts, and be beat with straps. Then they used to tie up a 28-pound [12.5 kg] weight to hang down our backs.

▼ **SOURCE 7** *This picture of pauper apprentices was originally an illustration for a book called* The Adventures of Michael Armstrong, Factory Boy, *published in 1840. It was written by Frances Trollope, one of the many people involved in the campaign to stop the employment of young children in mills. In 1840, after visiting several mills in Manchester and Bradford, she wrote her book based around the supposedly 'real life' but actually fictional experiences of Robert Blincoe. She was criticised at the time for writing about such a subject. One critic said that she should be sent to prison for writing such a dangerous book*

▼ SOURCE 8 *Leonard Horner, a government-appointed factory inspector, describes what happened to a young girl in a textile factory*

She was caught by her apron, which wrapped around the shaft. She was whirled round and repeatedly forced between the shaft and the carding engine. (Her right leg was found some distance away.)

▼ SOURCE 9 *A cartoon drawn by George Cruikshank. Cruikshank was against children working in factories. Sir Robert Peel was the politician chairing a Parliamentary Committee investigating working conditions in 1816. He was also a mill owner and Cruikshank is imagining an event at Peel's own mill*

▼ DISCUSS

1 It is clear that when Frances Trollope's fictional story (Source 7) and Cruikshank's cartoon (Source 9) were published they were against children working in mills. Does that mean we can learn nothing from them about children working in mills?
2 Does the accident described by Leonard Horner (Source 8) sound familiar to you? Where from?
3 Which of Sources 5–9 do you think is most likely to tell the truth about the mills?

▼ STORY WRITING

4 Use these two pages to record some historical notes in the plot box of your table.
5 Add any more story ideas you have had.

Parliamentary report

In 1830 Richard Oastler wrote a letter to the *Leeds Mercury* attacking the practice of children working in mills. He compared their treatment to the treatment of slaves.

From this point on the campaign against children working in mills gathered speed. In 1831 a Parliamentary Select Committee was set up. This Committee interviewed hundreds of witnesses and produced a report which painted a shocking picture of conditions in mills.

▼ **SOURCE 10** *Elizabeth Bentley, aged 23 in 1831, began work in a mill in Leeds when she was six years old*

Q. Explain what you had to do.
A. When the frames are full, they have to stop the frame, and take the flyers off, and take the full bobbins off, and carry them to the roller, and then put the empty ones on.
Q. Does that keep you constantly on your feet?
A. Yes, there are so many frames, and they run so quick.
Q. Suppose you flagged [tired] a little, what would they do?
A. Strap us. The girls had black marks on their skin many a time, and their parents dare not come to him [the overseer] about it; they were afraid of losing their work.
Q. In what part of the mill did you work?
A. In the card-room. It was very dusty. The dust got upon my lungs, I got so bad in health. When I pulled the baskets all heaped up they pulled my shoulder out of its place and my ribs have grown over it. I am now deformed.

▼ **SOURCE 11**
Jonathan Downe

When I was seven years old I went to work at Mr Marshall's factory at Shrewsbury. If a child was drowsy, the overseer touches the child on the shoulder and says, 'Come here'. In a corner of the room there is an iron cistern [tank] filled with water. He takes the boy by the legs and dips him in the cistern, and sends him back to work.

▼ **DISCUSS**

1 Read this source warning.

Critics of the report said that it had been stage-managed, that the witnesses had been asked deliberately leading questions. Certainly the witnesses had been coached in their answers and campaigners against child labour paid their expenses to go to the hearing.

2 Do you think Sources 10–14 are more or less likely to be true than Sources 5–9 on pages 26–27?
3 According to these sources what was wrong with the treatment of child workers? List at least three problems.

▼ **SOURCE 12**
David Rowland

Q. At what age did you commence working in a cotton mill?
A. Just when I had turned six.
Q. What employment had you in a mill in the first instance?
A. That of a scavenger.
Q. Will you explain the nature of the work that a scavenger has to do?
A. The scavenger has to take the brush and sweep under the wheels, and to be under the direction of the spinners and the piecers generally. I frequently had to be under the wheels, and in consequence of the perpetual motion of the machinery, I was liable to accidents constantly. I was very frequently obliged to lie flat, to avoid being run over or caught.

▼ SOURCE 13 *Eliza Marshall*

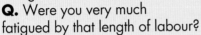

Q. What were your hours of work?

A. When I first went to the mill we worked from six in the morning till seven in the evening. After a time we began at five in the morning, and worked till ten at night.

Q. Were you very much fatigued by that length of labour?

A. Yes.

Q. Did they beat you?

A. When I was younger they used to do it often.

Q. Did the labour affect your limbs?

A. Yes, when we worked over-hours I was worse by a great deal; I had stuff to rub my knees; and I used to rub my joints a quarter of an hour, and sometimes an hour or two.

Q. Were you straight before that?

A. Yes, I was; my master knows that well enough; and when I have asked for my wages, he said that I could not run about as I had been used to do.

Q. Are you crooked now?

A. Yes, I have an iron on my leg; my knee is contracted.

Q. Have the surgeons in the Infirmary told you by what your deformity was occasioned [caused]?

A. Yes, one of them said it was by standing; the marrow is dried out of the bone, so that there is no natural strength in it.

Q. You were quite straight till you had to labour so long in those mills?

A. Yes, I was as straight as any one.

▼ SOURCE 14

John Hall, overseer

Q. Do you live at Bradford?

A. Yes.

Q. Are you the overseer of Mr John Wood?

A. I am.

Q. Will you have the goodness to state the present hours of working in your factory?

A. Our present hours are from six till seven.

Q. With what intervals for rest and refreshment?

A. Half an hour for breakfast and forty minutes for dinner.

Q. Do you believe that the children can endure the labour you have been describing without injury?

A. No, I do not.

Q. When your hands [children] have been employed for some time do you see any alteration in their appearance?

A. In the course of a few weeks I see a paleness in their faces, and they grow spiritless and tired.

Q. Have you remarked [noticed that] the cases of deformity are very common in Bradford?

A. They are very common. I have the names of, I think, about two hundred families I have visited myself that have deformed children, and I have taken particular care not to put down one single case where it might have happened by accident, but only those whom I judge to have been thrown crooked by the practice of piecing.

▼ ACTIVITY

1   You should now be able to use Sources 10–14 to add some final historical notes in the 'characters' and 'plot' boxes in your table.

2   Do you have more story ideas? If so, record them now.

▼ DISCUSS

3   Look back over your historical notes and story ideas. Talk about them with other people and help each other with ideas.

▼ STORY WRITING

4   Now it is time to write your short story. Don't forget the story recipe:

■ The year is 1819.

■ The events of your story happen inside a cotton mill.

■ Your story covers all or part of a single day shift, between 5 a.m. and 8 p.m.

■ Your story may have no more than three main characters.

Robert Owen: a better way to run a factory?

►► **History is never simple. The picture of poor children being badly treated was not true for all factories. One employer who thought that there was a better way to run a factory was Robert Owen.**

By the age of twenty Robert Owen was the manager of a large spinning mill in Manchester. In 1799 he bought some cotton mills in New Lanark, Scotland. He ran them very successfully. They made large profits.

Owen became convinced that he needed to improve conditions at New Lanark. He believed that if factory owners treated their workers better they would work better, and so the owners would make bigger profits. He also thought that by improving the environment and providing education he would improve the character of his workers.

He stopped employing children under ten, and educated them instead. He made many other improvements at New Lanark as you can see from Sources 1–3.

He wrote several books to publicise his work. He toured Britain making speeches on his experiments at New Lanark. He published his speeches as pamphlets and sent free copies to influential people in Britain. In one two-month period he spent £4000 publicising his activities. In 1816 he was summoned to Parliament to explain his ideas. Parliament liked them.

In 1819 Parliament passed a Factory Act to improve conditions in the mills. It banned children under nine years from working in factories. Children over nine years were allowed to work for only twelve hours. However, because of the opposition of other factory owners the Factory Act did not bring as many improvements as Owen wanted.

▲ **SOURCE 1** *A painting of the New Lanark Institute in 1825*

▼ **SOURCE 2** *From A New View of Society, written by Robert Owen in 1814*

When I arrived the workers possessed almost all the vices and very few of the virtues of a social community. Theft was their trade, idleness and drunkenness their habit . . . I formed my plans accordingly . . .

The system of receiving apprentices from public charities was abolished; permanent settlers with large families were encouraged, and comfortable houses were built for their accommodation.

The practice of employing children in the mills of six, seven and eight years of age was stopped, and their parents advised to allow them to acquire health and education until they were ten years old.

The children were taught reading, writing and arithmetic, during five years, that is, from five to ten, in the village school, without expense to their parents . . .

Those employed became hardworking, temperate, healthy, faithful to their employers, and kind to each other . . .

Owen was not above a little exaggeration either. His book and the picture in Source 1 were designed to spread his own ideas, so he may not always have told the whole truth.

▼ **SOURCE 3** *Evidence given by Robert Owen to Sir Robert Peel's House of Commons Committee on 26 April 1816*

Seventeen years ago, a number of individuals, with myself, purchased the New Lanark establishment. I found that there were 500 children, from poor-houses, from the age of five to eight. The working hours at that time were thirteen. Although these children were well fed their limbs were very generally deformed, their growth was stunted, and although one of the best schoolmasters was engaged to instruct these children regularly every night, in general they made very slow progress, even in learning the common alphabet. I came to the conclusion that the children were injured by being taken into the mills at this early age, and employed for so many hours; therefore, as soon as I had it in my power, I put an end to a system which appeared to me to be so injurious.

▼ **SOURCE 4** *Robert Owen (1771–1858)*

▼ **ACTIVITY**

1   **Make a list of all the improvements Owen made at New Lanark.**
2   **Use your list and the information and sources on this page to create a publicity leaflet for Owen to send to other factory owners. It should encourage them to adopt his methods.**

▼ **STORY REVIEW**

3   **Look back at your short story. How might it have been different if you had set it in Robert Owen's mills in 1826?**

Review: How did the Industrial Revolution change things?

▼ **REVIEW ACTIVITY**

The changes you have studied in this unit are all part of what historians call the INDUSTRIAL REVOLUTION. These are a complex set of changes which are all connected to each other. Maybe the best way to show this is to draw a big spider diagram. The diagram below is your starting point. Work with a partner to add as many elements to your diagram as you can.

Start by adding these items where you think they best fit:

- Wedgwood's fine china
- Arkwright's water frame
- water wheels
- child workers.

Then look back over pages 11–31 to find more ideas to add.

When you have finished keep your diagram handy – you may want to add other items to it later, as you find out more about the impact of the Industrial Revolution on Britain.

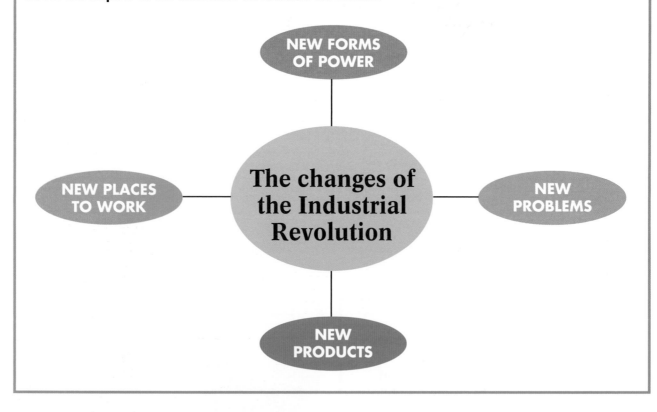

DEPTH STUDY 2

EMPIRE AND TRADE

The biggest empire!

Can you find the pink bits? They all belonged to Britain. In the 1800s Britain's was the biggest and richest empire in the world. It was said that 'the sun never sets on the British Empire.'

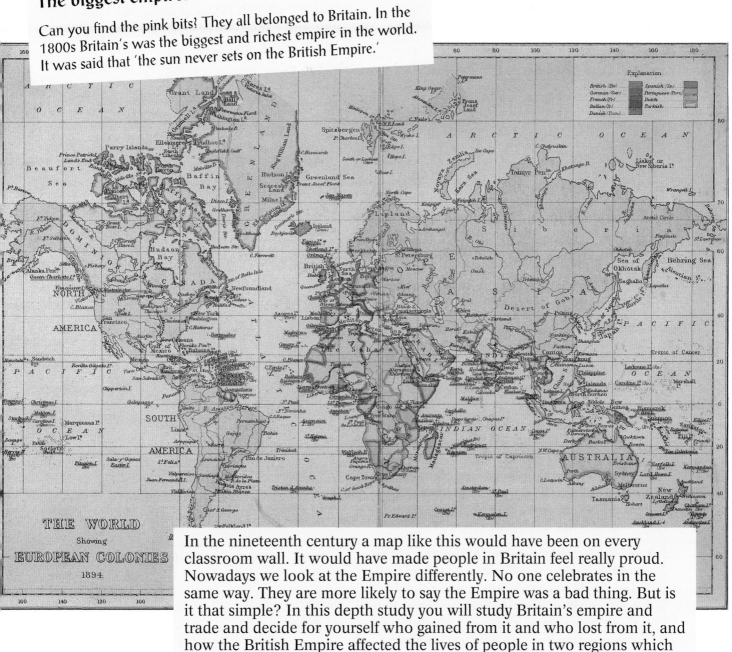

In the nineteenth century a map like this would have been on every classroom wall. It would have made people in Britain feel really proud. Nowadays we look at the Empire differently. No one celebrates in the same way. They are more likely to say the Empire was a bad thing. But is it that simple? In this depth study you will study Britain's empire and trade and decide for yourself who gained from it and who lost from it, and how the British Empire affected the lives of people in two regions which still have strong links with Britain today – the West Indies and India.

What was the British Empire for?

▶▶ In the nineteenth century everyone assumed that it was a good thing to have an empire. Nowadays it takes more explaining. So what was an empire for?

What was it?

Source 1 shows you all the countries in the British Empire. All these countries were ruled from Britain. They were called COLONIES. Some were simply countries where so many British people had settled that they had become British. Some had been 'won' in wars. Some had been 'discovered' and 'claimed' by British explorers.

How did the Empire help Britain?

The Empire was a great source of wealth to Britain. Britain got cheap raw materials from its colonies then sold the finished goods back to the colonies at a profit. Trade with other countries also grew. This made the merchants and factory owners huge amounts of money and provided jobs in British factories.

▼ DISCUSS

Imagine that Source 2 is the only piece of evidence you have about the British Empire.

1 Discuss with a partner all the things that it tells you about the Empire.

■ These might be things you are sure about – for example, facts which the source tells you.

■ They might be things that you can infer from the source. 'Infer' means to look beyond the obvious and work out something that is not actually stated. For example, why was the British Empire described as 'the Empire on which the sun never sets'?

2 Write your ideas down. At the end of this unit you will come back to this plate and see if you can explain it in more detail.

3 Look at either the pie charts on imports or those on exports in Source 1. Describe the changes you can see. Can you explain them?

How did the Empire help the colonies?

In many ways it did not help them at all. In fact most historians will say that the Empire kept the colonies poor. Others argue that British rule helped countries to develop and that the British brought peace and order. You will find examples of both aspects in this depth study.

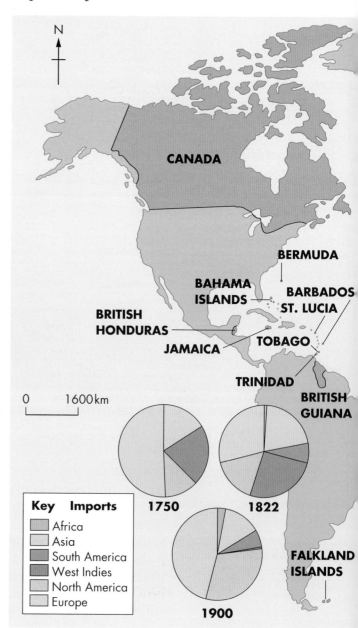

CANADA

BERMUDA

BAHAMA ISLANDS

BARBADOS
ST. LUCIA

BRITISH HONDURAS

TOBAGO

JAMAICA

TRINIDAD

BRITISH GUIANA

0   1600 km

1750

1822

FALKLAND ISLANDS

Key   Imports
Africa
Asia
South America
West Indies
North America
Europe

1900

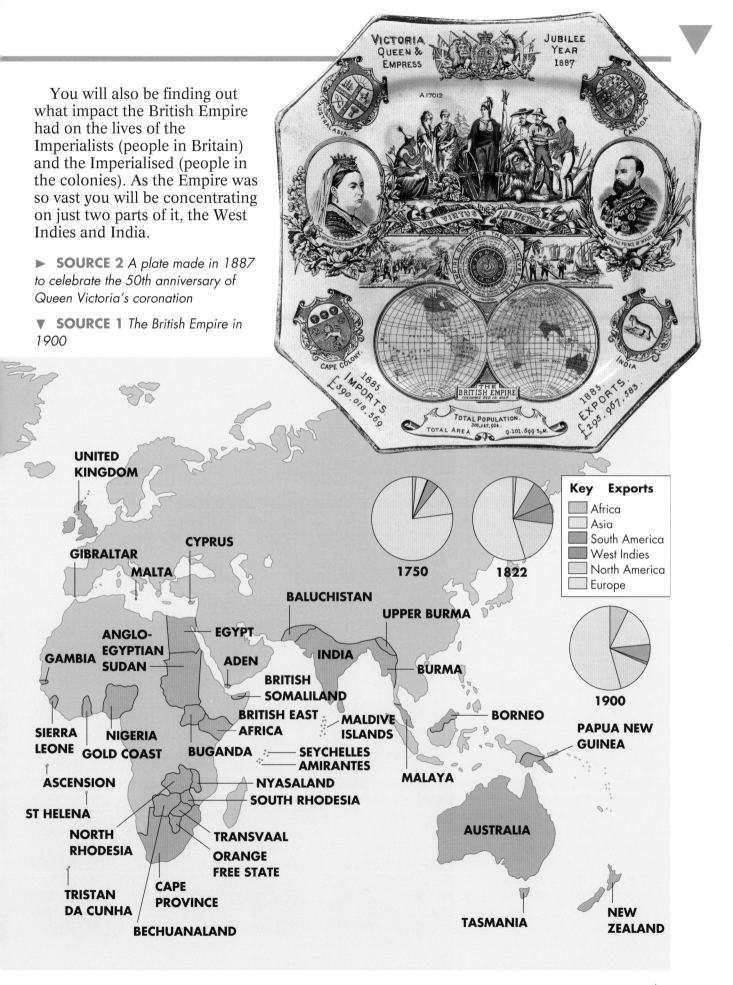

You will also be finding out what impact the British Empire had on the lives of the Imperialists (people in Britain) and the Imperialised (people in the colonies). As the Empire was so vast you will be concentrating on just two parts of it, the West Indies and India.

► **SOURCE 2** *A plate made in 1887 to celebrate the 50th anniversary of Queen Victoria's coronation*

▼ **SOURCE 1** *The British Empire in 1900*

VICTORIA QUEEN & EMPRESS

JUBILEE YEAR 1887

A 17012

AUSTRALASIA.   CANADA.

UBI VIRTUS   IBI VICTORIA

CAPE COLONY.   INDIA

THE BRITISH EMPIRE
COLOURED RED IN MAP

1885. IMPORTS. £390,018,569

1885. EXPORTS. £295,967,583.

TOTAL POPULATION. 305,347,924.

TOTAL AREA 9,101,699 S₂M.

UNITED KINGDOM

CYPRUS

GIBRALTAR

MALTA

BALUCHISTAN

UPPER BURMA

ANGLO-EGYPTIAN SUDAN

EGYPT

INDIA

BURMA

GAMBIA

ADEN

BRITISH SOMALILAND

BRITISH EAST AFRICA

MALDIVE ISLANDS

BORNEO

PAPUA NEW GUINEA

SIERRA LEONE

NIGERIA

GOLD COAST

BUGANDA

SEYCHELLES

AMIRANTES

MALAYA

ASCENSION

NYASALAND

SOUTH RHODESIA

ST HELENA

NORTH RHODESIA

TRANSVAAL

ORANGE FREE STATE

AUSTRALIA

TRISTAN DA CUNHA

CAPE PROVINCE

BECHUANALAND

TASMANIA

NEW ZEALAND

Key   Exports

- Africa
- Asia
- South America
- West Indies
- North America
- Europe

1750   1822

1900

35

Why does London need new docks?

▶▶ **It is 1800. Merchant William Armstrong has got problems. Let him tell you about them . . .**

In the eighteenth century Britain's trade went from strength to strength. Britain is now the world's wealthiest trading nation. London is the greatest port in the world, and London's docks are the busiest in the world. We IMPORT many items, tea, coffee, pepper, spices, silks, porcelain, timber, you name it. All these goods flood into London from overseas. Goods manufactured by Britain's new industries also flood into London, for EXPORT. The London docks are crammed with ocean-going ships.

Then there are the thousands of ships involved in the coastal trade between London and other parts of Britain. Bulky goods like grain, building materials or coal are usually brought to London by ship, even from Kent which isn't very far away at all. The amount of coal brought to London from Newcastle and Sunderland has tripled since 1700. So now the London docks are bursting at the seams with coal barges, timber barges, and thousands of smaller boats as well. All of these boats head for the Pool of London, the area between the Tower of London and London Bridge.

▶ **SOURCE 1** *The Pool of London early in the eighteenth century*

36 ▲

> The docks just cannot cope. There are not enough quays for boats to dock against, so they end up moored four or five abreast in midstream. Over 3000 small boats called 'lighters' continuously ferry the boats' cargoes to and from the quays. But this leads to long delays, which cost us merchants money. Also, because the quays are piled high with cargoes, the docks make easy pickings for thieves. We lose a lot of goods that way.
>
> What we need are new docks; deep-water docks for ocean-going ships, and plenty of warehouse space.

▼ **ACTIVITY**

In 1799 over 100 merchants set up a company to build new docks for the West Indies trade. Their plan was to use the docks themselves, and also to charge other merchants to use them.

Write a letter from William Armstrong to the government asking permission to build the new docks. Include a list of reasons why London needs new docks.

Britain's slave trade: the inside story

▶▶ **Britain's trade with the West Indies depended on SLAVERY. You are now going to investigate the tragic story of slavery in detail. Your aim is to prepare an anti-slavery campaign to inform the great British public about the 'inside story' of the slave trade.**

The case of the slave ship *Zong*

On 6 September 1781 the slave ship *Zong* sailed from the coast of Africa bound for Jamaica. On board were seventeen white crewmen and about 440 African slaves.

By the end of November the *Zong* was nearing Jamaica. By this time seven of the crew and more than 60 slaves had died. Many of the other slaves were badly ill. But instead of heading for Jamaica with all possible speed, Collingwood, the captain, started to sail in the opposite direction! He knew that when he reached Jamaica no one would want to buy the sick slaves. This would mean that the owners of the ship would lose money. Collingwood also knew that the slaves, like any ship's cargo, were insured, but that the insurance company would not pay up if the 'cargo' died from natural causes. So, if the slaves kept dying and more became ill, the owners would lose all their money.

Collingwood hit on what he thought was a brilliant idea. He called the ship's officers together to tell them about it. He said that if they threw the sick slaves overboard the owners would be able to claim money back from the insurance company. They could pretend that they were running out of drinking water and that they had to save the water for the fit slaves, who would then have a better chance of surviving. He also said that the sick slaves would be quickly put out of their misery.

After some argument the officers agreed and over the next few days 133 sick slaves were thrown overboard. Some of them put up a fight and were chained before being thrown overboard. Some, seeing what was going to happen, jumped overboard themselves rather than be thrown. One of the officers later stated that on 1 December, after 42 slaves had been thrown overboard, it rained heavily all day. It also emerged that when the *Zong* arrived in Jamaica on 22 December it had 420 gallons of water left.

The owners claimed the insurance money for the lost cargo on the grounds that the ship had run out of water so some of the slaves had to be killed in order to save the crew and the other slaves. The insurance company refused to pay and the case went to court.

▼ SOURCE 1 *From a speech by the owners' lawyer during the court case*

What is all this talk of human people being thrown overboard? This is a case of goods. It is a case about throwing over of goods. They are goods and property.

▼ ACTIVITY

Today this seems a deeply shocking story. Yet in the 1780s it raised hardly a murmur to start with because most people in Britain were very ignorant about the slave trade and many of those who knew the truth did not really care.

In this enquiry your task will be to prepare an anti-slavery campaign to make them care. Your campaign should tell the people of Britain the inside story of the evils of the slave trade. It could feature pictures, stories, leaflets or articles.

Condemning the slave trade will be easy with stories like that of the *Zong* to tell. But you need to do more than that. You need to present facts, so you must get your facts clear, otherwise your argument won't hold up.

Over the next ten pages you will do some careful research. You will make notes that you think might be useful for your campaign. Instructions like this will guide you:

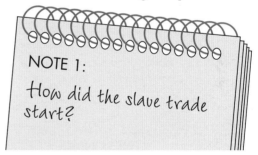

NOTE 1:
How did the slave trade start?

You will research:

■ how the slave trade started
■ why the slave trade was so profitable
■ how British people benefited from the slave trade
■ how the slaves were treated on the slave ships
■ how slaves were treated in the West Indies.

At the end you will use your notes to plan and present your campaign.

Remember the source warnings on pages 26–31? Watch out here as well. Most of the sources about slavery from the time were either prepared to support slavery or to criticise it, so look out for bias.

How did Britain's slave trade start?

The trade triangle

In the trade triangle (Source 2) ships never sailed empty and people made huge profits:

- the West African war lords who captured and sold the slaves
- the British slave traders who bought and sold the slaves. In the 1730s the average voyage from Bristol, picking up 170 slaves in Africa, made a profit of £8000 – an enormous sum of money in those days

- the PLANTATION owners in the West Indies who used slave labour to grow their crops – in 1780 the plantation owners in the West Indies supplied two-thirds of the cotton imported into Britain
- the factory owners in Britain, who had found a market for their goods – in 1770 one-third of Manchester's textiles were exported to Africa and half to the West Indies, where the cloth was used for blankets and clothes for the slaves.

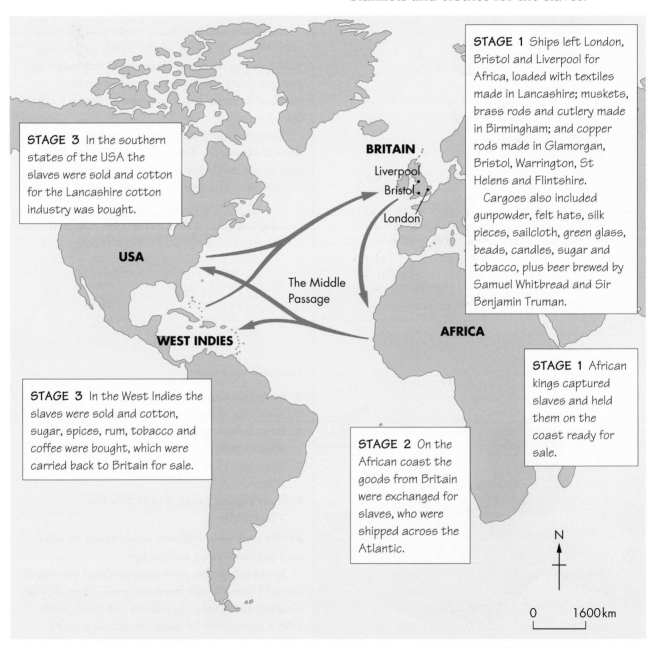

STAGE 1 Ships left London, Bristol and Liverpool for Africa, loaded with textiles made in Lancashire; muskets, brass rods and cutlery made in Birmingham; and copper rods made in Glamorgan, Bristol, Warrington, St Helens and Flintshire.

Cargoes also included gunpowder, felt hats, silk pieces, sailcloth, green glass, beads, candles, sugar and tobacco, plus beer brewed by Samuel Whitbread and Sir Benjamin Truman.

STAGE 3 In the southern states of the USA the slaves were sold and cotton for the Lancashire cotton industry was bought.

STAGE 3 In the West Indies the slaves were sold and cotton, sugar, spices, rum, tobacco and coffee were bought, which were carried back to Britain for sale.

STAGE 2 On the African coast the goods from Britain were exchanged for slaves, who were shipped across the Atlantic.

STAGE 1 African kings captured slaves and held them on the coast ready for sale.

BRITAIN

Liverpool
Bristol
London

The Middle Passage

USA

WEST INDIES

AFRICA

N

0   1600km

▲ **SOURCE 2** *The trade triangle*

Supply

In West Africa in the 1500s slavery was a part of normal life. Prisoners of war were taken as slaves. Slaves were a king's status symbol. He had to look after them and clothe them. He owned them – they worked for him.

plus Demand

Meanwhile European explorers settled in the Americas. In the West Indies they grew sugar and cotton and found an easy market for these goods in Europe. They could sell as much as they could grow! So now they needed workers for the sugar and cotton plantations. Slaves were their answer.

equals The slave trade

Plantation owners bought slaves from kings in West Africa and sailed them over to the West Indies as forced labour.

Growth

This development changed the African slave trade. Instead of just capturing slaves for their own use, new powerful, warrior kingdoms such as the Ashante and Dahomey emerged. Their whole aim was to capture other Africans to sell them to the Europeans. They were well armed (with guns made in Europe) and the demand for slaves was massive. As demand went up so did prices and so did the slave catcher's profits.

Disaster for West Africa

The slave trade spelled disaster for West Africa. For three centuries the healthiest young people of the region were taken away. No-one is sure exactly how many men, women and children were sold into slavery but probably about 11 million African people were landed in the Americas between 1500 and 1850. Add to that the number who died in war or en route, and the devastating effect on families who lost their loved ones or their bread-winner, and you can begin to see the impact on life in West Africa.

Profit for Britain

By the 1700s British traders led the international slave trade. A trade triangle (see Source 2) had grown up which made British traders, African kings and British plantation owners very rich indeed. The slave trade was the most important and the richest part of Britain's trade in the eighteenth century.

▼ ACTIVITY

1 **Study the chart above and make your first notes about how the slave trade started.**

NOTE 1:

How did the slave trade start?

a) the role of African kings

b) the role of plantation owners

2 **Study Source 2 then make notes about why the slave trade was so profitable.**

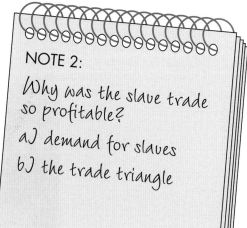

NOTE 2:

Why was the slave trade so profitable?

a) demand for slaves

b) the trade triangle

How did Britain benefit from the slave trade?

One of the most important cities involved in the trade triangle was Liverpool.

In 1700 Liverpool was a small sea port with a population of 5000. In 1709 Liverpool slave traders set out on their first voyage to buy and sell slaves. By 1771 there were 106 ships a year sailing from Liverpool, which between them carried 282,000 slaves. Half of Liverpool's sailors were involved in the slave trade. In the 1790s Liverpool's slave trade alone accounted for fifteen per cent of Britain's entire overseas trade. By 1800 Liverpool was a successful, booming city of 78,000 people.

Workers

The slave trade provided many jobs in Liverpool. By 1774 there were eight sugar refineries and fifteen rope factories. There were many factories making chains, anchors, and iron, copper and brass goods for the slave ships.

Bankers

Money poured into Liverpool from the slave trade. Banks did well by lending money to traders, but slave merchants also used their profits to set up Liverpool's most important banks. In the 1780s Liverpool made a profit from the slave trade of over £1 million a year. The trade was so profitable that it was not just the rich who wanted to be part of it. Many tradespeople bought a share in a slave ship.

▼ **SOURCE 3** *Written by Malachy Postlethwayt, a Liverpool trader, in 1746*

The extensive employment of our shipping to and from America, and the daily bread of most of our British manufacturers, are owing mainly to the labour of Negroes.

The Negro trade is the main source of wealth and naval power for Britain.

▶ **SOURCE 4** *Liverpool in 1680*

▶ **SOURCE 5** *Liverpool in 1830*

Ordinary people

Thousands of ordinary people in the rest of Britain depended on slavery too. Some people worked in factories or used railways which had been set up with slave trade money. For example, Thomas Harris, a Bristol slave trader, helped set up an iron works in South Wales.

Nearly 20,000 people worked in industries which sold their goods to West Africa in exchange for slaves. Their jobs depended on slavery. Sugar provided jobs in England too – there were 120 sugar refineries providing thousands of jobs. Every person in Britain who used sugar benefited (and most people did). Sugar was added to bread, porridge, puddings and the new fashionable drinks coffee and tea. Britain was fast developing a sweet tooth – and losing its teeth as a result! Slave labour made sugar affordable.

▼ **DISCUSS**

Sources 6 and 7 give different views about the slave trade.

1 Explain how they differ.
2 Suggest possible reasons why they differ.

▼ SOURCE 6 *Written by a historian, J.F. Nicholls, in 1881*

There is not a brick in Bristol that was not cemented with the blood of a slave. Sumptuous mansions and luxurious living was made from the sufferings and groans of the slaves bought and sold by Bristol merchants.

▼ SOURCE 7 *From a history of Liverpool written by the city's public librarian and paid for by the city to celebrate the 750th anniversary of the city's charter in 1950*

In the long run, the triangular trade operation based at Liverpool was to bring benefits to all, not least to the transplanted slaves, whose descendants have subsequently achieved in the New World standards of education and civilisation far ahead of their countrymen whom they left behind.

Racism

Racism is a modern word, but it describes an ancient attitude – that people of another race from you, or another colour, are inferior. Many Europeans believed that white people were superior to blacks and that white people had a right to do as they wished with black people. The slave trade fed off this racist attitude, although as you see greed and ignorance were also important factors too!

▼ **ACTIVITY**

Make notes about how Britain benefited from the slave trade.

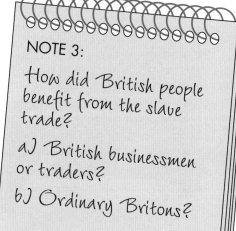

NOTE 3:

How did British people benefit from the slave trade?

a) British businessmen or traders?

b) Ordinary Britons?

▶▶ **You should by now have an idea of the importance of the slave trade. On pages 44–49 you are going to look at the human cost of this trade – the suffering of the slaves. Although many people in Britain benefited from slavery, they had little idea of how the slaves were treated.**

On the slave ships

Slaves were captured from inland areas then marched to the coast. At the coast they were sold to the slave traders who loaded them onto ships.

You will already know something about the conditions on the slave ships from the story of the *Zong* on page 38. Sources 8–11 tell you more.

Conditions on the slave ships

When you study evidence such as Sources 10 and 11 about the conditions on slave ships you will not be surprised that so many slaves fell ill.

You should also think of the ship out on the sea, rolling around on the waves. The slaves would be terrified and many would be seasick or have DYSENTERY. The lavatory was often a large bucket 60 centimetres across and 75 centimetres deep. Many of the slaves could not reach it, so the floor was soon filthy.

The ship owners wanted the slaves to be in good condition when they reached the West Indies, so the slaves were probably fed as well as was possible in the circumstances.

▲ **SOURCE 8** *An eighteenth-century illustration of slaves being packed below decks for the Atlantic crossing*

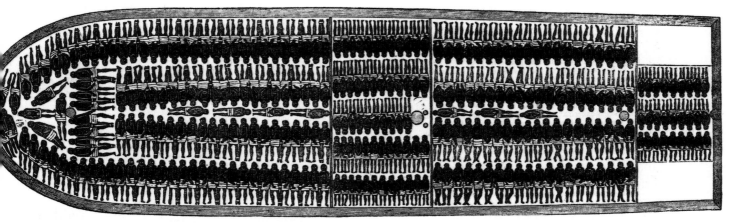

▲ **SOURCE 9** *A plan of the interior of a Liverpool slave ship. It was drawn by Thomas Clarkson, who campaigned to abolish the slave trade. The picture is quite accurate. As you can see, every space is filled*

▼ **SOURCE 10** *Written by Alexander Falconbridge, a surgeon who served on a number of slave ships*

The floor was covered with blood and mucus and resembled a slaughterhouse. After fifteen minutes I was so overcome by the heat, stench and foul air, that I nearly fainted. With assistance I got back on deck.

The slaves' meals consist chiefly of horse beans, boiled to a pulp; of boiled yams and rice, and sometimes a small quantity of beef or pork. They sometimes have a sauce of palm oil, mixed with flour, water and pepper.

On board some ships, the common sailors are allowed to have intercourse with such of the black women whose consent they can get. The officers are allowed to indulge their passions among them as they like, and sometimes are guilty of such brutal excesses as disgrace human nature.

▼ **SOURCE 11** *Written by an ex-slave trader, John Newton, in his* Journal of a Slave Trader, *written in 1788*

The poor creatures, thus cramped for want of room, are likewise in irons, for the most part both hands and feet, and two together, which makes it difficult for them to turn or move, to rise or lie down, without hurting themselves.

Twice a day a small bucket of food was handed to each group of ten slaves. The slaves usually had to scoop the food out with their hands. When the weather was good they might be fed on deck.

Some of the slaves simply gave up the struggle to stay alive and refused to eat. Others committed suicide. Slave revolts on ship were common, especially soon after leaving the coast of Africa. By the end of the eighteenth century the death rate amongst slaves during the voyage was about 55 per cent.

Most ships carried some women slaves. They were kept, unchained, in the smaller spaces between the decks, with the child slaves.

▼ **ACTIVITY**

Use Sources 8–11 and the story of the *Zong* to make notes about conditions on the slave ships.

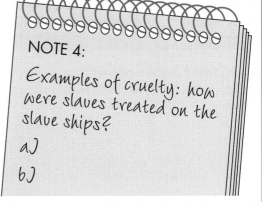

NOTE 4:

Examples of cruelty: how were slaves treated on the slave ships?

a)

b)

On the plantations

British people knew virtually nothing of the life that the slaves led on the sugar plantations in the West Indies. Sources 12–22 on pages 46–49 give us an impression of this life.

A slave sale

When the slave ships reached the West Indies the slaves were cleaned up ready to be sold. One ship's captain, who had a batch of slaves suffering from dysentery, told the doctor to block the anus of each slave with rope.

▶ **SOURCE 12** *A poster advertising a sale of slaves alongside household goods and a horse*

TO BE SOLD & LET

BY PUBLIC AUCTION,

On **MONDAY** the 18th of **MAY, 1829,**

UNDER THE TREES.

FOR SALE,

THE THREE FOLLOWING

SLAVES,

VIZ.

HANNIBAL, about 30 Years old, an excellent House Servant, of Good Character.

WILLIAM, about 35 Years old, a Labourer.

NANCY, an excellent House Servant and Nurse.

The MEN belonging to "LEECH'S" Estate, and the WOMAN to (Mrs. D. SMIT

TO BE LET,

On the usual conditions of the Hirer finding them in Food, &c. and Medical

THE FOLLOWING

MALE and FEMALE

SLAVES,

OF GOOD CHARACTERS.

ROBERT BAGLEY, about 20 Years old, a good House Servant.

WILLIAM BAGLEY, about 18 Years old, a Labourer.

JOHN ARMS, about 18 Years old.

JACK ANTONIA, about 40 Years old, a Labourer.

PHILIP, an Excellent Fisherman.

HARRY, about 27 Years old, a good House Servant, used to House Work and the Nursery.

LUCY, a Young Woman of good Character, used to House Work and the Nursery.

ELIZA, an Excellent Washerwoman.

CLARA, an Excellent Washerwoman.

FANNY, about 14 Years old, House Servant.

SARAH, about 14 Years old, House Servant.

Also for Sale, at Eleven o'Clock,

Fine Rice, Gram, Paddy, Books, Muslins, Needles, Pins, Ribbons &c. &c.

AT ONE O'CLOCK, THAT CELEBRATED ENGLISH HORSE,

BLUCHER,

ADDISON, PRINTER, GOVERNMENT

▲ **SOURCE 13** *A nineteenth-century print of a slave family being auctioned*

▼ **SOURCE 14** *A description by Olaudah Equiano, who was sold as a slave and later became a leading campaigner against the slave trade*

On a given signal the buyers rushed at once into the yard where the slaves are confined, and made choice of that parcel that they liked best. The noise and clamour increased the worry of the terrified African. In this manner are relations and friends separated, most of them never to see each other again.

Work

After the sale, most of the slaves were immediately taken to work on sugar plantations.

▼ **SOURCE 15** *A contemporary description of plantation work in 1807*

The slaves are divided into three classes called gangs; the first of which consists of the most healthy and strong, both of the males and females, whose chief business is, before crop time, to clear, hoe, and plant the ground; and during crop time to cut the canes, feed the mills, and attend to the manufacture of the sugar.

The second gang is composed of young boys and girls and pregnant females who weed the canes and do other light work.

The third gang consists of younger children, attended by an old woman, who collect green food for the pigs and sheep and weed the garden.

▼ **SOURCE 16** *A painting from 1823 showing a white overseer supervising field slaves cutting sugar cane*

▼ **SOURCE 17** *The slaves' day*

 5.30 a.m. Go to fields taking their breakfast with them, register called, then work till 8.00 a.m.

 8.00–8.15 a.m. Breakfast: boiled yam, eddoes, okra, all seasoned with salt and pepper. Any latecomers arriving are whipped.

 8.15a.m–12.00 noon. Work.

 12.00 noon–2.00 p.m. Rest and dinner: salted meat or pickled fish.

 2.00–6.00 p.m. Work.

6.00 p.m. Return to their huts.

 6.00pm–5.30 a.m. Sleep. However, during the harvest season work in the mill and boiling houses continued throughout the night.

Punishments

The hard life and the lack of freedom sometimes led to slave revolts. There were over 30 rebellions in the West Indies in the period 1750–1850. These rebels were severely punished.

▼ **SOURCE 18** *A report by a visitor to a plantation in Jamaica in the eighteenth century*

The punishments are:

For rebellions, burning them by nailing them down on the ground with crooked sticks on every limb, and then applying the fire by degrees from the feet and hands, burning them gradually up to the head, whereby their pains are great.

For crimes of a lesser nature, gelding [castrating] or chopping off half of the foot with an axe.

For running away, they put iron rings of great weight on their ankles, or pothooks about their necks, which are iron rings with two long hooks riveted to them, or a spur in the mouth.

For negligence, they are usually tied up and whipped by the overseers.

▲ **SOURCE 19** *A modern photograph of a man wearing a neck ring, which was worn by slaves as a punishment 24 hours a day*

▲ **SOURCE 20** *A cartoon from 1791 commenting on the treatment of slaves in the West Indies*

Health

The slaves' poor diet, living conditions and hard work all led to a life expectancy (the average age at death) of only 26. The death rate among babies was particularly high: 25 per cent of all babies died of tetanus before they were ten days old. Smallpox, measles and whooping cough could all be fatal too. Nobody bothered to register a baby's birth until it had survived for several weeks.

◄ **SOURCE 21** *Treadmills like this were introduced to the West Indies as an 'improved' form of punishment*

▼ **SOURCE 22** *An advertisement for a runaway slave in the* Jamaica Royal Gazette, *1782*

MARIA, a washer, bought from James Elford, the initials of whose name she bears on one of her shoulders – she eloped in October and has been seen in Port Royal.

▼ **ACTIVITY**

From the text and sources on pages 46–49 make final notes about how the slaves were treated in the West Indies.

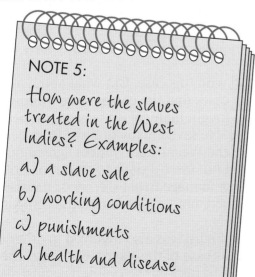

NOTE 5:

How were the slaves treated in the West Indies? Examples:
a) a slave sale
b) working conditions
c) punishments
d) health and disease

It is now time to plan your campaign.
You could:

■ write an illustrated article for a national newspaper
■ create an exhibition
■ design a poster or a leaflet.

You could include:

■ interviews
■ stories
■ pictures.

Think about how you could use the story of the *Zong* to create impact.

You might also get more ideas for your campaign from the pictures and sources on the next four pages which are about the actual campaign against slavery which was launched in Britain in the late 1700s.

Why was slavery abolished?

In 1807 the slave trade was abolished by the British Parliament. It became illegal to buy and sell slaves, but people could still *own* them. In 1833 Parliament abolished slavery itself, making it illegal to own slaves in Britain and throughout the British Empire.
Why did this happen, when the slave trade and the plantations in the West Indies seemed to be making so much money? As you will see there is not a simple answer to this question.

FACTOR 1 The white campaigners

If you had been reading this book 30 years ago the explanation for the abolition of slavery would have seemed simple. The authors would have told you that as people in Britain learned about the awfulness of the slave trade they were appalled. Their good nature and their sense of right and wrong won over and they persuaded Parliament to ban slavery. In this explanation it is the white campaigners who appear to deserve all the credit. Here are some key features of their campaign.

The abolition of slavery was achieved through the efforts of the white campaigners.

Granville Sharp: campaigner

A chance meeting started one of the greatest campaigners against slavery on his work. As Sharp left his house one day in 1765 he noticed a black youth queuing for free medical help. His head was badly swollen, he was nearly blind and he could hardly walk. His name was Jonathan Strong and he told Sharp that he had been brought to Britain as a slave and had been beaten up by his owner, so he had run away.
Sharp took Jonathan Strong to a hospital, where he gradually recovered. Two years later he was healthy and working as a messenger boy. But one day his old master saw him, had him captured and sold him. Strong would be taken back to Jamaica as a slave. Granville Sharp took the case to court, where the Lord Mayor of London ruled: 'This lad has not stolen anything, and is therefore at liberty to go away.'
Sharp had won this case. But what about all of the other similar cases that the courts were waiting to hear? Sharp fought many of these cases on behalf of black people. He saved many of them from being sent back to the West Indies. Judges agreed that a master could not force a slave to go out of Britain. Sharp did not manage to get slavery or the slave trade abolished, but he had started the campaign against slavery.
Granville Sharp was also involved in other court cases, such as case of the slave ship *Zong*. These cases helped to turn public opinion against slavery.

▼ ACTIVITY

1 Make your own large copy of this diagram.
2 In each circle put your explanation of how this factor helped to abolish slavery. Give examples or evidence to support this explanation.
3 On the arrows write your explanation of how one factor linked to or helped the others.
4 Write a paragraph to explain what your diagram shows and stick it underneath the chart. Begin your paragraph 'There are different reasons why slavery was abolished. This diagram shows that . . .'

FACTOR

FACTOR   FACTOR

The Society for the Abolition of the Slave Trade

The Society was set up in 1787. Many of its leaders were QUAKERS, who believed that slavery was sinful and against Christian teaching.

William Wilberforce is the best-known member of the Society. He was an MP and made many speeches in Parliament against the slave trade.

Another member, Thomas Clarkson, collected together all the information he could about the terrible conditions on the slave ships. This included interviewing an estimated 20,000 sailors. He used his findings to persuade people of how awful the trade was. Source 9 on page 45 is taken from his research.

Huge petitions were collected and presented to Parliament. For example, in Manchester in 1788 over 10,000 working people signed a petition and in 1792 over 20,000 signed another petition (this was out of a population of 75,000). Huge protest meetings were held all over the country.

Again and again the campaigners tried to get Parliament to abolish the slave trade. In 1807 they finally succeeded.

But the campaign did not stop there. It continued, with the aim of making slavery illegal and freeing all existing slaves. In 1814 1.5 million people signed petitions in support of the abolition of slavery. In fact, more people signed these petitions than signed the famous CHARTIST petitions in the 1840s which demanded reform of Parliament (see pages 92–97).

▶ **SOURCE 1**
Josiah Wedgwood, the owner of Britain's most famous potteries, made thousands of plaques like this. He even sent a shipload to the USA. The caption reads 'Am I not a man and a brother?'

▼ **SOURCE 2** *Extracts from a speech by Prime Minister William Pitt in a debate in the House of Commons in 1792 about the abolition of the slave trade*

I know of no evil that ever has existed worse than the tearing of 70,000 or 80,000 persons each year from their native land. If we tempt the slave traders to sell their fellow creatures to us we may rest assured they will use every method – kidnapping, village breaking, bloodshed and misery – to supply their victims to us.

Think of 80,000 persons carried away out of their own country. Do you think nothing of their families which are left behind?

▼ **SOURCE 3** *An extract from a speech at a working-class meeting in Sheffield*

Slavery is insulting to human nature. Its abolition will redeem the national honour, too long sullied by the trade of blood, and promote the cause of liberty. It will avenge peacefully ages of wrongs to our negro brothers.

FACTOR 2 Black people's actions

The slave trade brought thousands of Africans to Britain – by 1800 there were an estimated 10,000 black people living in Britain. The first breakthrough came when black slaves in Britain tried to free themselves. They demanded to be treated like ordinary servants. Some demanded wages. Many others ran away.

Often the slave's owner went to court to get the slave back, but the legal position of slavery in Britain was never clear. There was no law that said slavery was legal in Britain but there was no law that said it was illegal. When slaves claimed their freedom in courts in Britain the judges seemed to make a different decision every time!

Granville Sharp (see page 50) helped many of these slaves to fight their cases in the courts. Increasingly, the law courts did set them free. Soon it was not worth the trouble for slave owners to chase down their escaped slaves. By 1800 most black people in Britain were free.

> Think again. Black people freed themselves by their own actions, by running away, by rebelling and by campaigning on their own behalf.

▼ **SOURCE 4** *A complaint about black slaves by an English magistrate in 1768*

They no sooner arrive here than they put themselves on a footing with other servants, become intoxicated with liberty, and begin to expect wages.

Olaudah Equiano: campaigner

When he was just ten years old Olaudah Equiano was taken from Africa to Barbados as a slave. He worked as a servant to a ship's captain and so he travelled widely. He stayed in London for some time, where he learned to read and became a Christian. He hoped that he would be made free, but his master took him to America and sold him. However, Equiano eventually bought his freedom and returned to England, where he married Susan Cullun from Ely.

In 1789 he wrote the story of his life. This was widely read and turned many people against slavery. He travelled the country speaking at meetings and worked closely with other abolitionists like Granville Sharp. In fact it was Equiano who brought the case of the slave ship *Zong* (see page 38) to the public's attention. He died in 1797.

▶ **SOURCE 5** *A portrait of Olaudah Equiano*

Slave revolt!

Slave revolts had happened throughout the period of the slave trade. For example, there were 16 slave rebellions in Jamaica between 1655 and 1813. In the late 1700s the most serious revolt led to major change on one West Indian island: St Domingue, a French colony in the West Indies. The conditions for slaves on St Domingue were among the worst in the West Indies. The death rate was very high because of the dreadful treatment they received.

In 1791 the slaves rebelled, murdering plantation owners and setting fire to the sugar cane fields. British troops were brought in to help the French regain control, but the slaves, brilliantly led by a slave called Toussaint L'Ouverture, defeated them.

Slavery was abolished, and in 1804 the island declared itself independent with the new name of Haiti.

All over the West Indies, plantation owners lived in terror of further slave revolts.

▲ **SOURCE 6** *A slave revolt*

FACTOR 3 Economics

> You are both missing the point. It was economics that did it. It's no coincidence that Britain abolished slavery just when it became clear that slavery was no longer making a profit.

From the 1770s onwards the West Indies were becoming less important to Britain. Cuba and Brazil could produce cheaper sugar. Many plantations in the West Indies were closed down. The demand for slaves fell. For example, in 1771 Barbados imported 2728 slaves, but in 1772 none were imported. It became clear to plantation owners that it was cheaper to employ ex-slaves as waged labourers than to own slaves who you had to house and feed. With a smaller market for their cargoes there was less profit for the slave traders in the West Indies.

▼ **SOURCE 7** *Written by the economist Adam Smith in 1776*

The experience of all ages and nations, I believe, demonstrates that the work done by slaves, though it appears to cost only their maintenance, is in the end the dearest of any. A person who can acquire no property can have no other interest but to eat as much and to labour as little as possible. Whatever work he does can be squeezed out of him by violence only.

Britain and India: joined by a thread

▶▶ **The Indian leader Mohandâs Gandhi described India and Britain as being 'joined by a thread'. He actually meant 'cotton'. On pages 54–59 you are going to try to trace that thread.**

The East India Company

The East India Company was founded in England in 1599 and soon began building trading DEPOTS in India. India was not a united country. There were many small states, each with its own ruler. The East India Company sometimes established itself with the permission of these local rulers, sometimes without. To protect it's trade the Company had its own private army.

Meanwhile, the French had their own East India Company. Rivalry between the British and French was very intense, and in the 1700s it escalated into full scale war. In theory, these were wars between rival Indian states but the East India Company armies fought alongside the Indian armies.

For the British the aim was clear: to help any Indian ruler who would help them trade and defeat any ruler who blocked their trade – to control India for their benefit.

In 1757 Robert Clive persuaded an Indian general, Mir Jafar, to fight with him to overthrow Mir Jafar's own ruler, Siraj-ud-Daula, the Nawab of Bengal, at the Battle of Plassey. Clive won. After the battle Siraj was captured and executed.

This gave the Company control of Bengal and was a turning point in the British takeover of India. Clive was treated as a hero in England. In 1765 he was sent back to India to govern Bengal. From then on he took more and more Indian states under British control and the French were defeated. The British took over the administration of each Indian state they controlled and British people held all the top jobs.

◀ **SOURCE 1** *Robert Clive meeting Mir Jafar after the Battle of Plassey. Mir Jafar was an Indian general in charge of the Bengal army. Clive persuaded Mir Jafar to join him and together they plotted to overthrow the rule of Siraj-ud-Daula. Painted by Francis Hayman c. 1762*

INDIA

▼ **SOURCE 2** *A biography of Robert Clive, 'Clive of India'*

1725 Born in Shropshire

1743 Entered the service of the East India Company as a clerk

1744 Arrived in Madras, India

1748 Joined the Company's army

1751 A small force under his command seized Arcot, and then held it against attack from far greater numbers; this made his military reputation

1757 Victory at Plassey over Siraj-ud-Daula paved the way for British control of India

1760 Returned to Britain and was given a hero's welcome

1765 Returned to India to govern Bengal

1767 Ill health forced him to return to Britain; he was accused of corruption, having made himself very rich whilst in India

1773 Parliamentary enquiry into his governing of Bengal found that it had not been corrupt and passed a motion saying that he had given 'great and meritorious service to this country'

1774 Suffering from ill health and in great pain, despite taking opium, he committed suicide

▼ **SOURCE 3** *Map showing the British takeover of India*

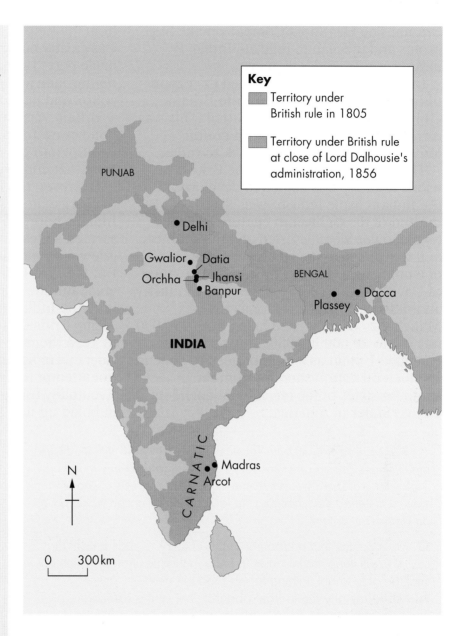

Key

- Territory under British rule in 1805

- Territory under British rule at close of Lord Dalhousie's administration, 1856

PUNJAB

Delhi

Gwalior • Datia
Orchha • Jhansi
• Banpur

BENGAL

Plassey • Dacca

INDIA

CARNATIC

• Madras
Arcot

N

0   300km

Controlling cotton

Control of India produced great wealth for Britain. The East India Company made huge profits and it began to regulate Indian industry to Britain's advantage.

In 1800 the Company stopped the export of Indian silk and cotton cloth to Britain. Only raw cotton could be exported. This was turned into cloth by the British cotton industry and then exported back to India.

The result of this was that the British textile industry was helped to develop whilst the Indian textile industry was destroyed. By the end of the eighteenth century Indian textile towns were deserted and the spinners and weavers had moved elsewhere in search of employment. For example, the population of Dacca, once a centre of the textile industry and described by one visitor as the Manchester of India, had fallen from 450,000 in 1765 to 20,000 in 1800. This policy also benefited Britain as it did not need to depend so much on cotton supplies from the southern states of the recently independent United States of America.

Some Indians of the ruling classes benefited from the Empire but for most Indians the result was greater poverty. The Indian people were made poor. Labourers became dependent on renting land and growing CASH CROPS such as cotton and jute for export to Britain.

Britain was aware of the impact of its policies on India. In 1840 they conducted an enquiry into poverty in India. Source 4 comes from that enquiry.

However, the British government did little to change the system that was keeping the Indians poor. To the Indian people this seemed a great injustice. There were other grievances too, as you can see from Source 6. But the East India Company's control was so great and their army so strong that there was little the Indian people could do about it.

The British also cleverly used local rivalries to keep themselves strong: as long as Indian rulers were fighting each other they would not attempt to fight against British rule. Eventually though, in 1857, the resentment bubbled up into full-scale rebellion.

▼ **SOURCE 4** *Extract from Thomas Cope's interview with the House of Commons Select Committee set up to investigate poverty in India in 1840. He was a silk weaver from Macclesfield and was giving his view of the effect that changing the laws on Indian cotton would have on weavers in Britain*

Q. Do you think that a labourer in this country . . . has a right to say, we will keep the labourer in India in that position in which he shall be able to get nothing for his food but rice?

A. I certainly pity the Indian labourer, but at the same time I have greater feeling for my own family than I have for the Indian labourer's family. I think it is not good government to take away our labour and give it to the Indian, just because his condition happens to be worse than ours. It would make us unemployed, and throw us upon the rest of society to support us by charity. I hope this will never take place in this country.

▼ **DISCUSS**

Think about the following statements and decide whether they are true or false. Collect evidence to support your view.
a) 'The British Empire was good for the British cotton industry.'
b) 'The British Empire was bad for the Indian cotton industry.'

Why did the Indian army mutiny in 1857?

The East India Company's army was vital to British control of India. Most of its soldiers were Indian. In the 1850s they were unhappy for many different reasons. Source 6 on page 58 sums up their reasons for resentment. In particular they feared that the British were trying to convert them to Christianity. This resentment came to a head in May 1857 when the army was given new rifles.

Trigger

The new Lee Enfield rifles had greased cartridges. The end of each cartridge had to be bitten off before it could be loaded. The rumour was that the grease was made from the fat of pigs (abhorrent to Muslims) or cows (sacred to Hindus). The Indian soldiers refused to handle the cartridges and when they were forced to do so they mutinied, taking over army buildings, capturing equipment and imprisoning their British officers.

Spread

The mutiny soon spread through the army of Bengal. Troops seized Delhi and proclaimed the return of the ancient rulers of India. They declared their grievances in their rebel manifesto (see Source 7). Fighting continued throughout the year. Both sides did some terrible things; both sides killed men, women and children. The British finally defeated the Indian forces late in 1858.

After their victory the British executed some mutineers by firing them from cannons (see Source 5).

Consequence

Afterwards there was an enquiry into who was at fault. The East India Company was blamed and the India Act of 1858 ended its share in the government of India. From then until independence in 1947 the British government governed India directly – but still to Britain's advantage.

▼ **SOURCE 5** *The execution of the mutineers*

▼ **SOURCE 6** *Indian resentment against British control*

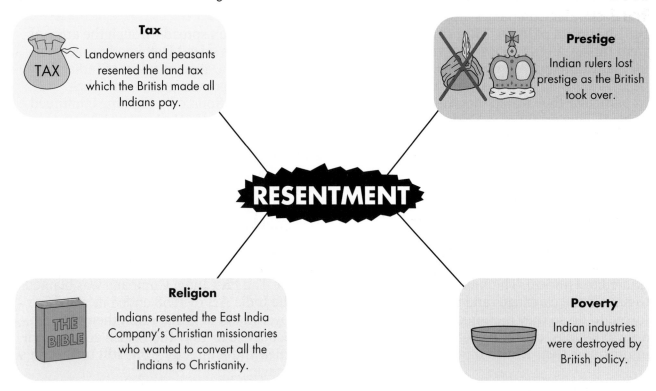

Tax
Landowners and peasants resented the land tax which the British made all Indians pay.

Prestige
Indian rulers lost prestige as the British took over.

RESENTMENT

Religion
Indians resented the East India Company's Christian missionaries who wanted to convert all the Indians to Christianity.

Poverty
Indian industries were destroyed by British policy.

▼ **SOURCE 7** *An extract from the 'Rebel Manifesto' printed in the Delhi Gazette, September 1857*

Section 2 Regarding Merchants
It is plain that the infidel and treacherous British government has monopolised the trade of all the fine and valuable merchandise . . . leaving only the trade in trifles [items of little value] to the people, and even in this they are not without their share of the profits, which they secure by means of customs and fees, etc. . . . So that the people have merely a trade in name.

Section 3 Regarding Public Servants
It is not a secret thing, that under the British government, natives employed in the civil and military services have little respect, low pay, and no manner of influence; all the posts of dignity . . . are exclusively bestowed on Englishmen.

Section 4 Regarding Artisans
It is evident that the Europeans, by the introduction of English articles into India, have thrown the weavers, the cotton dressers, the carpenters, the blacksmiths, and the shoemakers etc., out of employ . . . every description [sort] of native ARTISAN has been reduced to beggary . . .

▼ **DISCUSS**

The British called this event a mutiny (when soldiers refuse to obey orders of their officers and try to take over leadership of the army). Others would call it a revolution (when people in a country try to change the way it is governed). Which do you think is the best description? Why?

Case study: Lakshmi Bai, Rani of Jhansi

On 6 June 1857 the Indian mutiny spread to Jhansi. Indian troops mutinied. They massacred 60–70 Europeans who had surrendered to them. Some people blamed Lakshmi Bai, the RANI of Jhansi, for this but she herself was threatened by the mutineers and was forced to give them money before they left for Delhi. After they left she took over the running of the kingdom and wrote to the British Commissioner asking for British troops and orders about what to do! He asked her to manage the kingdom on behalf of the British government.

However the British sent no troops. Now the story gets really complicated! Her neighbours, the Chiefs of Orchha and Datia, took advantage of the troubles. They invaded, saying that they were acting on behalf of the British. So the Rani raised troops, including some who had been mutineers. She allied with the RAJA of Banpur and she defeated the invaders. The Raja of Banpur was a leading rebel, so to the British this looked as though the Rani had joined the rebels, although she wrote to the British asking for help as late as January 1858. She may have been trying to 'keep a foot in both camps'.

In April 1858 the British attacked and captured her walled city of Jhansi. She led the defence, then escaped disguised as a man. She was now firmly on the side of the rebels and became one of their main leaders fighting against the British on a number of occasions. In June 1858, when riding as a horseman in male clothing, she was killed in a cavalry skirmish outside the city of Gwalior.

In later year she became a cult heroine of Indian nationalists. In the years 1905–1910 her image was taken out on floats during the religious festival of Ramlila. During the Second World War, Indian women anxious to fight with the Japanese against the British formed the Rani of Jhansi regiment in 1943.

▲ **SOURCE 8** *Lakshmi Bai*

▼ **ACTIVITY**

Gandhi said that India and Britain were joined by a thread.

1 Copy the thread drawing in your book (or use a real thread if you prefer).
2 Label it to show one of the connections between India and Britain.
3 Draw another thread and label it with another connection.
4 Draw and label as many more threads as you can using all that you have read about on pages 54–59.

BRITAIN

Review: Who benefited from the Empire?

▼ REVIEW ACTIVITY

This plate is going to be part of a museum exhibition about nineteenth-century Britain.

You have been given the job of writing an explanation to go with the exhibit.

Using all that you have found out about the Empire over the past 27 pages you should explain:

a) what the British Empire was

b) why people in Britain celebrated the Empire

c) why some people resented the Empire.

You don't need to present your explanation in writing. It could be a recording on an audio cassette, a question and answer panel, or an annotated copy of the plate, for example. Think of good exhibitions that you have been to and try to copy their presentation ideas.

DEPTH STUDY 3

TOWNS

The dirtiest town!
Would you like to live here? What if you had to – could you bear it? Why would anyone bear it?

In 1750 most people in Britain lived in small villages. By 1900 most lived in cities and towns like this one. This change is one of the biggest in this period.

In this depth study you will find out why people moved to the towns and cities and what life was like when they got there.

Foul facts!

One thing that everyone knows about Victorian towns is that they were foul places to live. But just how foul were they? And is that the whole story? Read on and decide for yourself.

▼ **SOURCE 1** *Ten foul facts on vile Victorian towns*

Ten foul facts on vile Victorian towns

1 All the sewage of Cambridge used to flow into the river, which made it a pretty disgusting place to walk beside. In 1843, Queen Victoria was walking beside the river when she asked one of the university teachers an embarrassing question.

2 In 1853 a cholera epidemic in London killed 11,500. London's drains carried sewage and germs straight into the river Thames. The river water was then used for washing clothes and even cooking! The Thames was such a stinking sewer in the hot summer of 1858 that the blinds of the Houses of Parliament had to be soaked in chloride of lime so that the MPs could meet without choking on the smell.

76

▼ **ACTIVITY**

The page in Source 1 comes from *The Vile Victorians*, one of the titles in the 'Horrible Histories' series written by Terry Deary and illustrated by Martin Brown. It shows the first two foul facts. Your task is to research, write and illustrate another eight. It is up to you to decide what these should be. You will find plenty of ideas to help you on pages 63–65.

Pollution

By the 1860s nearly all workshops and factories were powered by coal-burning steam engines, so the tall chimneys belched out smoke all day, every day. Coal was also used for heating houses and for cooking. This household smoke made the air pollution even worse.

▼ **SOURCE 2** *An engraving of Manchester in 1867. People live in the houses on the left. The building on the right is a cotton mill*

▼ **SOURCE 3** *Population figures (in thousands) of four towns that you are going to investigate in this depth study*

	1750	**1821**	**1901**
Brighton	–	24	123
Liverpool	35	138	685
London	675	1,504	4,563
Manchester	45	126	645

Overcrowding and disease

So many people moved to the towns that there were not enough houses. Builders and landlords, who were keen to make large profits, built thousands of new houses but they crowded as many as possible in and often used the cheapest building materials. Rents were high so whole families lived in a single room. Sometimes they even took in lodgers to earn extra money. There was little privacy. Infectious diseases spread easily.

▼ **SOURCE 4** *A cartoon called 'A Court for King Cholera' published in* Punch *magazine, 1852*

Rubbish

In many towns there was no effective system for collecting rubbish. The piles of rotting rubbish in courtyards and streets were breeding grounds for disease.

Sewage

This was a major problem as most houses were built without sewers or toilets. Usually the houses shared a privy, which might be built over a stream or, more likely, a cesspit. Since many cesspits were not lined, the sewage could seep into the water supply. As the pits were not regularly emptied they often overflowed, particularly in wet weather. They stank and were also a breeding ground for disease.

Damp

Housing for the poor was often badly built. With earth floors, single brick walls and poor roofing materials, the houses were damp.

Poor ventilation

With houses built so close together it was difficult to get either fresh air or light into the rooms.

Drinking water

Most houses did not have piped water. People had to get water from cisterns, stand pipes, wells, streams or rivers. The waste of the town polluted all of these. This meant that water-carried diseases like CHOLERA could easily spread.

Cleanliness/Hygiene

As it was hard to get water, people found it difficult to wash themselves, their clothing, their bedding and their cooking things. Many people had body lice. Food storage was a problem too. These were ideal conditions for killer diseases like typhus, typhoid and diarrhoea to flourish. One famous victim was Prince Albert, Queen Victoria's husband, who died from typhoid in 1861 at the age of 42. Even royalty and the rich were not safe from disease.

▼ **ACTIVITY**

▲ **SOURCE 5** *An engraving of city slums by Gustave Doré*

You should now be an expert in spotting foul facts. On a copy of this picture (which your teacher will give you) add labels to explain what foul facts you can see.

Were they pushed or were they pulled?

Meet the Chapman family: John and Mary are the parents; Annie, Ben and Victoria are the children. They are leaving their village and heading for the town. If we could read their minds what might they be thinking?

This is a new start for us all. There was no future for me in the village. The population's grown so fast that there aren't enough jobs to go round.

Not that I'd want those farming jobs. You work all day for a pittance – tiny wages. I've seen men who work all their lives and when they are old it's off to the WORKHOUSE with them – they have nothing to show for all that work.

And to cap it all you have to bow and scrape to his lordship every time you see him as if he's some sort of god.

Not my style. Not at all.

But the town – that's different. There are jobs in the town. They are well paid, and I'll be my own man.

My brother Samuel moved to town last year and he's done all right. He's foreman in the cotton mill already.

Maybe I'll do the same.

Yes, our Samuel has done well. He's even saved up some money – which is more than you can do in the village.

Samuel will look after us. He's already got a room and he says we can stay with him until we find our own.

▼ ACTIVITY

1 **Work with a partner. Study the thought bubbles carefully and write down all the different reasons why the Chapmans are moving to the town.**

2 **Now try to sort those reasons into two columns:**

   ■ **PUSH (bad things about the village which are pushing the family away)** *or*
   ■ **PULL (good things about the town which are attracting them). Some reasons will not fit into either column.**

3 **Write down what you imagine the youngest child, Victoria, might be thinking.**

There are some big changes coming up. I hope they are for the best.
John will be fine, but I worry about the children. The town's big and dirty. But we'll bear it if we have to. We have no choice really if we want to get somewhere in life. All the rich families in town need servants. It won't be long until Annie is old enough to go 'into service' for them.
She'll still be able to go to Sunday school so she will learn to read and write – she should do well.
I'll earn some money too. I can take in sewing or washing from all the factory workers. Samuel says they don't have time to do it themselves and will pay someone else to do it for them. Annie and Ben can help me.

I'll sell matchboxes or shine shoes. I wonder if Mum will still make me go to Sunday school? Dad says there is much more opportunity in the town.

Mum says I can become a servant – I'm not sure what I think about that. It sounds like very hard work, but it's what most girls are expected to do. Anyway I'll get paid and if I'm lucky I'll find a nice family to take me and live in a comfortable house – even if it's only in the attic.

Why did Liverpool and Manchester need a railway?

▶▶ **In the 1820s Liverpool and Manchester were two of the most important cities in England. Liverpool was a very busy port (see page 42). Manchester was the main centre of the quickly expanding cotton industry. But travel between the two was expensive and slow. On pages 68–73 you will explore why there was this problem, how it was solved and how people reacted.**

The problem

This picture shows you the methods of transport between Liverpool and Manchester in 1820.

Raw materials for Manchester were piling up at the Liverpool docks. Sometimes they might be there for weeks. There were not enough canal barges. There were hold-ups at the locks. The canal companies were charging very high rates. Because there was more than enough traffic to keep all of the routes busy all of the time, the canal companies did not have to compete with each other by setting low rates.

By road

By 1800 the 36-mile (58 km) road from Liverpool to Manchester was packed with waggons and packhorses – 70 packhorses left one Liverpool inn in a day! Passengers had 22 regular coaches a day. The journey took three hours. The road was looked after by a number of TURNPIKE TRUSTS, but it was often in a very poor condition.

Rates for transporting goods between Liverpool and Manchester:

- all goods 40s a ton

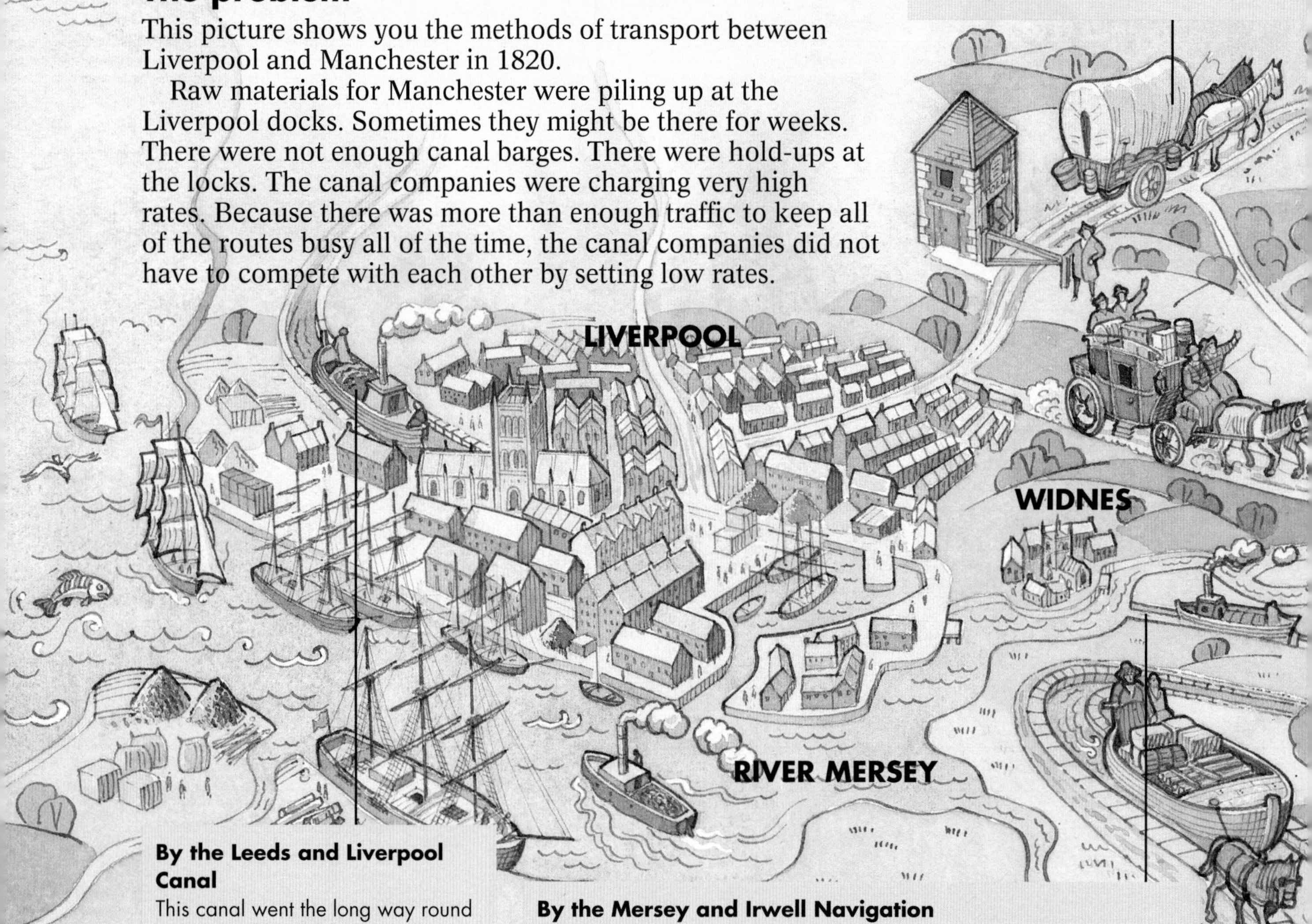

LIVERPOOL

WIDNES

RIVER MERSEY

By the Leeds and Liverpool Canal

This canal went the long way round – 58 miles (91 km) had to be travelled. It was particularly used for carrying bulky goods such as coal, brick, lime and timber. The journey took up to three days.

Rates for transporting goods between Liverpool and Manchester:

- all goods 9s 2d a ton

By the Mersey and Irwell Navigation

This had made the two rivers navigable. It was 43 miles (69 km) long. It carried imported goods such as cotton and sugar, and home-produced goods such as grain, stone, timber and coal. On the lower part of the Mersey, as it approached the sea, boats could be delayed by tides, wind and storms. Higher up, at the Manchester end, they could be held up by lack of water in the Irwell. The journey often took 36 hours.

Rates for transporting goods between Liverpool and Manchester:

- cotton 20s a ton
- grain 13s a ton
- sugar 16s 8d a ton

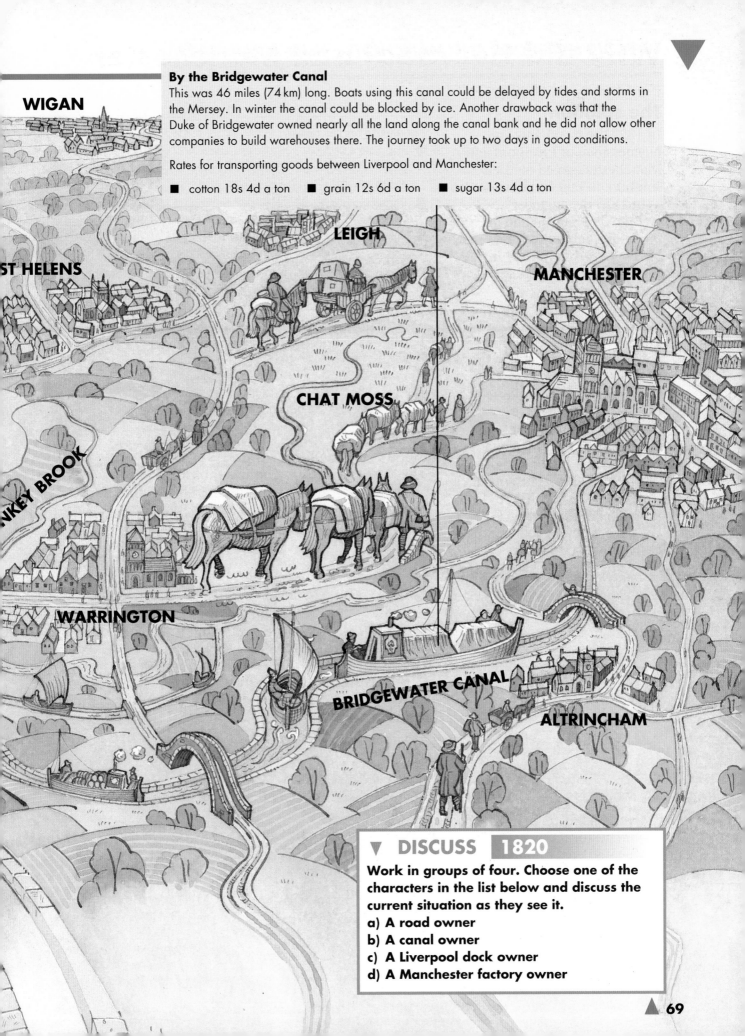

WIGAN

ST HELENS

LEIGH

MANCHESTER

CHAT MOSS

NKEY BROOK

WARRINGTON

BRIDGEWATER CANAL

ALTRINCHAM

By the Bridgewater Canal

This was 46 miles (74 km) long. Boats using this canal could be delayed by tides and storms in the Mersey. In winter the canal could be blocked by ice. Another drawback was that the Duke of Bridgewater owned nearly all the land along the canal bank and he did not allow other companies to build warehouses there. The journey took up to two days in good conditions.

Rates for transporting goods between Liverpool and Manchester:

- cotton 18s 4d a ton   ■ grain 12s 6d a ton   ■ sugar 13s 4d a ton

▼ **DISCUSS** 1820

Work in groups of four. Choose one of the characters in the list below and discuss the current situation as they see it.
a) **A road owner**
b) **A canal owner**
c) **A Liverpool dock owner**
d) **A Manchester factory owner**

The solution

In 1822 the merchants and businessmen of Liverpool and Manchester agreed on their solution: to build a railway.

In 1825 the engineer George Stephenson had been the brains behind the first passenger steam railway in England, between Stockton and Darlington.

The businessmen had heard about Stephenson's work. They invited him to be the engineer for the Liverpool and Manchester Railway.

To build a railway was a major undertaking. You needed masses of money. You needed local support. Then you needed a creative and determined engineer to make a plan. Hardest of all, you needed permission from Parliament before you could begin any work.

Arguments for the railway
- The owners of mines in St Helens would be given a direct link with Liverpool and could export their coal all over the world.
- Farmers would be able to send their produce to market more quickly and cheaply.
- Manufactured goods and raw materials would be carried for half the cost of canal travel in one-sixth of the time.
- The railway would be more reliable than the canal because a canal could be closed by frost, drought, wind and tide, goods got damaged by the water, and there were not enough barges.
- The cost of coal in Liverpool would go down.
- Passengers could travel more quickly and cheaply.

Stage 2: raising local support

The next job was to win the support of the local people.

The local industrialists and merchants prepared their arguments for the railway. Leaflets, posters, letters to the press and public meetings were used to present their point of view. They wrote to local MPs and even elected the Mayor of Liverpool as Chairman of the Company to get the support of the Council.

Those people opposed to the railway also got themselves organised with leaflets and letters to the press. The opposition was led by powerful local landowners: the Earls of Derby and Sefton, and the Duke of Bridgewater. They all owned land along the planned route. When Stephenson and his men tried to survey the route they were turned off the land and even attacked. They ended up carrying out the survey at night by torchlight!

Stage 1: raising money

In 1824 the Liverpool and Manchester merchants formed the Liverpool and Manchester Railway Company. The estimated cost of building the railway was £300,000, so the company issued 3000 SHARES which people could buy at £100 each. If the railway was successful the shareholders would get some of the profits. Lots of people wanted to invest in the company. They thought the railway would be very successful.

Stage 3: getting Parliament's permission

By 1825 the survey was done, the best route was chosen and the costs were worked out.

But the Company could not just go out and build a railway. Parliament had to give permission.

Various groups sent petitions to Parliament for and against the railway. In 1825 Parliament began to debate the plan for the railway.

Some of those sending petitions to Parliament in support of the railway
- Corn merchants in Cork and Dublin, in Ireland
- Liverpool merchants in the West Indian and East Indian trade
- the Liverpool Ship Owners' Association
- Merchants, manufacturers and traders of Leeds, Bradford and Dewsbury

Some of those sending petitions to Parliament against the railway
- the Earls of Derby and Sefton
- the owners of the Leeds and Liverpool Canal
- the owners of the Bridgewater Canal Company
- Smaller landowners along the railway route
- Barton Road Turnpike Trustees
- the Mersey and Irwell Navigation Company

Arguments against the railway
- Hunting would be ruined.
- Cows would not graze within sight of the locomotives.
- Women would miscarry at the sight of the locomotives.
- Farm land, crops and buildings would be burned and destroyed by sparks from the steam locomotives.
- At massive speeds of up to ten miles per hour the train would leave the track or shake the goods and passengers to pieces.
- Smoke and soot would get into people's houses and gardens in Liverpool and Manchester.
- The canal and road businesses would be ruined.

▼ **DISCUSS** 1825

In groups of four choose one of the characters from the list on page 69 and decide if they would be for or against the plans for the railway. What would they have said to support their argument? You can get some ideas from the bullet points on these two pages.

How was the railway built?

Parliament rejected the plan.

One important reason for this was that the Company insisted that steam locomotives, rather than horses, should be used to pull the trains.

So in 1826 the Company decided to present a new plan to Parliament. It made changes to the old plan so that there would not be so much opposition.

The route was changed:

- to avoid much of the land of the Earls of Derby and Sefton
- to leave Liverpool by tunnel so no streets had to be crossed
- to stop on the edge of Manchester rather than going right into the centre.

Other changes were made as well:

- The question of whether or not to use steam engines was left open.
- Canal owners were offered shares in the railway (so they could share in any profits).

This time Parliament said 'yes'. The building could begin.

Fares were also fixed by Parliament. Cotton would cost 9s 6d per ton for the journey.

Stephenson had to plan and then build embankments, cuttings, bridges, engines and machinery. Sources 1–4 show how he solved the various problems that he faced.

The Company decided to use a steam locomotive rather than horse power. It ran some trials at Rainhill to decide which locomotive to use. In October 1829 about 15,000 people turned up to watch Stephenson's 'Rocket' win the trials. It went at 15 miles per hour when pulling stones and passengers and at 28 miles per hour without. The public were stunned at the speed.

▲ **SOURCE 1** NAVVIES at work on the 30-metre deep Olive Mount cutting

◀ **SOURCE 2** The entrance to the 2-kilometre tunnel into Liverpool at Edgehill. Navvies had to bore through two kilometres of solid rock

▼ SOURCE 3 *The Sankey Viaduct, which was built to carry the railway over the Sankey Brook*

▼ SOURCE 4 *Cross-section of the railway on Chat Moss*

Stephenson used 200 men to cut four parallel drains to drain water away and dry a 14-metre strip of the moor

To make a good foundation for the railway track Stephenson put down moss and brushwood to form an embankment, then covered it with earth, sand and gravel, followed by a coating of cinders, then the track

Was the railway a success?

The railway opened in September 1830. There were six trains a day. The journey took an hour and 40 minutes. Each train carried about 120 passengers as well as goods. The impact was immediate.

▼ SOURCE 5 *From the annual register in 1832, two years after the railway opened*

All the coaches have stopped running. The canals have reduced their prices by 30 per cent. Goods are delivered in Manchester the same day as they arrive in Liverpool. The saving to manufacturers in Manchester, in the transporting of cotton alone, has been £20,000 a year. Coal pits have been sunk and factories established along the railway, giving greater employment to the poor. The railway pays one-fifth of the poor rates in the parishes through which it passes. The transportation of milk and garden produce is easier. Residents along the line can use the railways to attend their business in Manchester and Liverpool with ease and little expense. No inconvenience is felt by residents from smoke or noise. The value of land on the line has gone up because of the railway. It is much sought after for building.

▼ SOURCE 6 *Travel on the new railway*

	Passengers	Goods (tons)	Coal (tons)
1830	71,951	1,433	2,630
1835	473,847	230,629	116,246

The biggest surprise was the large number of passengers who used the railway. It was clear to everyone that a railway powered by a steam locomotive to carry people was practicable and profitable. It led to a furious boom period of railway building as cities and towns all across Britain got their own railway. The era of fast and cheap passenger transport had finally arrived. Towns spread, suburbs grew, and cheap seaside holidays were discovered. But that is another story which you will investigate in the next enquiry . . .

▼ DISCUSS 1835

In groups of four take the characters you chose for 1820 (page 69) and 1825 (page 71). What would they be saying about the Liverpool–Manchester railway in 1835?

Beside the sea!

In 1750, Brighton was a small town. By 1900 it had changed completely. In this enquiry you will investigate these changes.

1825: An upper-class resort

In 1750 Dr Richard Russell, a Brighton doctor, published a book called *The Use of Sea Water in Diseases of the Glands*. He argued that drinking seawater and bathing in it were good for health. Wealthy people started to go to Brighton to follow his advice.

In 1783 the Prince of Wales went to Brighton for the first time. He liked the town and built the spectacular Royal Pavilion.

The royal interest established Brighton as a fashionable place to visit. From 1800 it was mainly a resort for the wealthy upper classes. 'Assembly rooms' were created where ladies and gentlemen could meet, eat and dance together.

Swimming in the sea was popular. Men and women had to swim from separate parts of the beach. 'Bathing machines' (wooden huts on wheels) were used for changing in, and were wheeled into the sea before the bather came out. The men swam naked.

▼ **SOURCE 1** *A cartoon by George Cruikshank called* Mermaids at Brighton, *1820*

▼ **SOURCE 2** *The Royal Pavilion in Brighton, designed to look like an Indian palace and completed in 1821*

Sake Deen Mahomed

Sake Deen Mahomed was a famous Brighton businessman. He was born in India in 1749, and came to Britain with a British army officer for whom he had worked in India. He moved to Brighton to set up his business – 'warm, cold and vapour baths'. He also introduced the practice of 'shampooing'.

In order to overcome white people's prejudice against him, he offered to treat influential clients without charge. This proved very successful, and he soon had many customers. The King gave him the title 'Shampooing Surgeon to His Majesty George IV' and put him in charge of the baths at the Royal Pavilion.

In 1822 Mahomed wrote a respected medical book. It described the many patients he had treated successfully. It included cures for asthma, rheumatism, sciatica, lumbago and loss of voice.

▲ **SOURCE 3** *Sake Deen Mahomed*

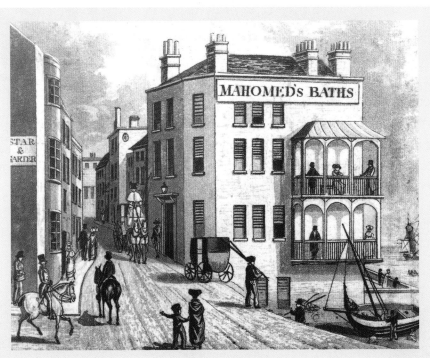

◄ **SOURCE 4** *A nineteenth-century picture of Mahomed's Baths*

▼ **SOURCE 5** *A description of the baths written by a modern historian, Rosina Visram, in 1986*

The patients first lay in a steaming aromatic herbal bath; having sweated freely, they were then placed in a kind of flannel tent with sleeves. They were then massaged vigorously by someone outside the tent, whose arms alone penetrated the flannel walls.

▼ **ACTIVITY**

Draw up a chart like the one below.

Brighton in 1825	Brighton in 1850

Fill in column 1 of your chart with all the features that you can find on pages 74–75.

1850: a popular resort

All over the country the coming of the railways brought seaside resorts within the reach of ordinary people. London was the biggest city in the world: when the London–Brighton railway opened in 1841, millions of people were suddenly only two hours' train ride away from the seaside. For the first time, the 'day tripper' appeared in Brighton. In 1837 stage-coaches had taken 50,000 travellers to Brighton in a whole year. In 1850 the railway carried 73,000 in one week.

To start with it was mainly middle-class visitors who went to Brighton. To cater for them large hotels were built. As the town grew, industries developed alongside the holiday trade, and slums developed too.

In the late nineteenth century many working-class holiday-makers began to go to Brighton as well. The middle classes and working classes preferred holidays in the summer, so the upper classes tended to go in the autumn and winter when the town was less crowded.

▼ **SOURCE 6** A cartoon from Mr Punch at the Seaside *called 'A Quiet Drive by the Sea'*

▼ **SOURCE 7** The Chain Pier in 1833. It was originally built for passengers to get on and off the steamboats that ran along the coast. But the public could pay 2d to walk on it. More money was raised from people walking on the pier than from the steamer passengers. Later, shops and performers began to work on the pier

▲ **SOURCE 8** *A painting called* To Brighton and back for 3s 6d. *The stage coach fare had been £1 and the journey took all day. The train cost 3s 6d. It left at 7.00 a.m. and arrived in Brighton at 9.00 a.m.*

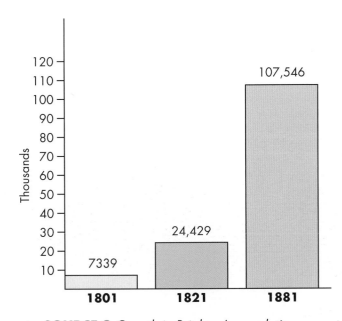

▲ **SOURCE 9** *Growth in Brighton's population*

▼ **ACTIVITY A**

1   Use pages 76–77 to record as many features as possible in the 1850 column of your chart from page 75.

▼ **DISCUSS**

Compare your 1825 and 1850 lists.

2   How has Brighton changed?
3   Are these changes for the better or for the worse? Why?
4   What different factors led Brighton to change in the early 1800s?
5   How was the arrival of the railway in 1841 a turning point in Brighton's history?

▼ **ACTIVITY B**

6   Use the information in your chart to design an advert to attract visitors to Brighton in either 1825 or 1850. Give your advert a headline, an illustration and some bullet points or text presenting the town's best features.

The different faces of London

▶▶ In 1900 London was the largest city in the world. It was the heart of the British Empire, the largest empire in the world. Some people thought that London represented the pinnacle of human achievement; others thought it was ghastly! See who you agree with after you have read pages 78–83.

▼ ACTIVITY

It is 1900. You are in charge of attracting people to London. Some of you are in charge of attracting workers. Some have to attract tourists. After splitting into groups, decide which group of people you are aiming at and use the information and sources on pages 78–83 to help you design a brochure to attract them.

1 First of all, think about how the two brochures should be similar and how they should be different.

2 Gather information for your brochure from pages 78–83. If you find something that would be more useful for another group, tell them about it.

3 You could do other research of your own to find out more about London at this time.

4 Choose no more than two pictures for your brochure.

5 Use ICT to create your final brochure.

The imperial capital

To a visitor in 1900 London must have been an incredible sight. There were magnificent new buildings, including the Houses of Parliament, new bridges over the River Thames, and great museums such as the Natural History Museum in Kensington. There were also magnificent new railway stations, such as St Pancras and Paddington. They were the size of cathedrals and just as grand, and included vast hotels with hundreds of rooms.

The Houses of Parliament and St Pancras Station (Source 1) were both built in the popular Gothic style. This deliberately copied the architecture of medieval churches.

Most of the trade of the Empire passed through London. It had a vast system of docks (see pages 36–37).

▼ **SOURCE 1** *St Pancras Station and Hotel. The railway companies built hotels for their passengers above their main-line stations*

The entertainment capital

The entertainment and leisure industry grew along with the population. By 1900 London had more than 80 theatres and 90 music halls which offered non-stop singing, dancing and comedy acts. The first cinemas had opened showing 'silent' films. Film studios had been set up in Ealing. Regent's Park Zoo had opened in 1847, and Twickenham Rugby Stadium in 1860. The first cricket 'test' matches were played at Lord's cricket ground in the 1880s. Football clubs sprang up all around London. The new stadium at Crystal Palace could hold 100,000 spectators.

▶ **SOURCE 2**
Crystal Palace stadium in 1905

▼ **SOURCE 3** *The Theatre Royal, Drury Lane, one of the oldest and grandest of London's 80 theatres. Tickets cost more than a day's wage*

The commuter capital

Developments in transport had changed the face of London for ever. As the railways grew, London grew with them (see Source 6). Lower middle-class workers (such as clerks or shop workers) could now live on the outskirts of the city, in suburbs, where cheap housing was built (see Source 5). The government made the railway offer low fares to workers so that they could afford to travel into London to work. The first underground railway was opened in 1863 (see Source 4) and two more were opened by 1900.

▼ **SOURCE 4** *The Metropolitan Railway, London's first underground railway, opened in 1863. It was steam-powered until it was electrified in 1905*

▼ **SOURCE 5** *Housing built in 1875*

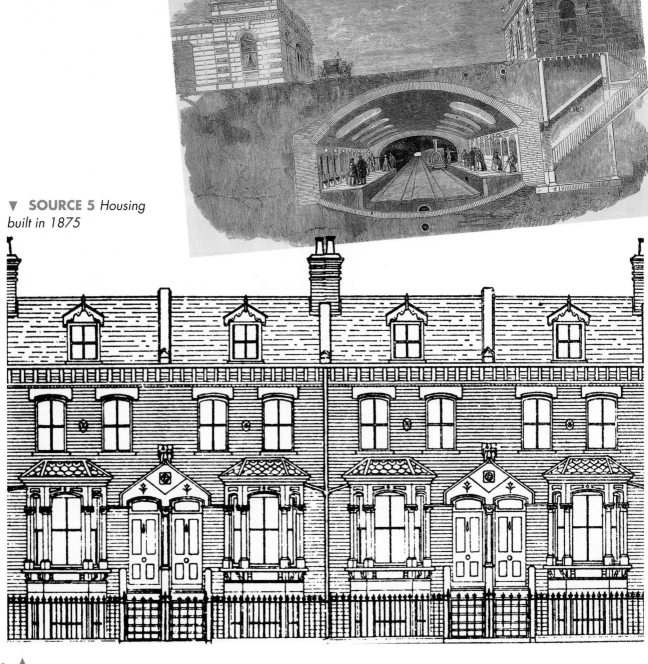

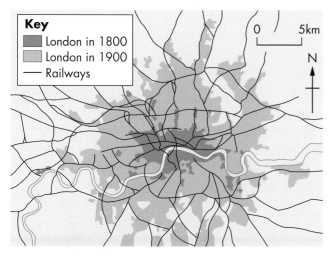

0   5km

N

▲ **SOURCE 6** *The growth of London 1800–1900*

▼ **SOURCE 7** *Industries in West Ham in 1900*

Leather cloth works   Guano works
Distillery   Dye works
Iron works and shipyard   Marmalade factory
Docks and warehouses   India rubber works

The work capital

The choice of jobs in London was vast. The city was firmly established as the centre of world banking and finance. The docks employed hundreds of thousands of people. But London also had thousands of small industries. Source 7 lists the industries in one small area of London. Most of these industries processed goods that came in through the London docks.

There were also new factories appearing, including those making new products such as electrical goods or motor vehicles. Most of the new industries were built in the east of the city because they needed to be close to the docks.

The better housing for the rich and middle classes was built in the west or the south. This was because the prevailing winds carried the pollution from the city centre towards the east.

▼ **SOURCE 8** *People also travelled in from the suburbs to shop in the massive new department stores*

HARRODS LTD. LONDON, S.W.

The most elegant & commodious EMPORIUM in the WORLD.

The slum capital

In 1880 Charles Booth, a rich businessman, moved to London to open a branch of his shipping business. He was very impressed by the aspects of London mentioned on pages 78–81, but he was appalled by the slums he saw in the East End of London, near to the docks. He decided to tell everyone in Britain about the terrible conditions he saw. His team of assistants visited every house in the area and in 1889 he published his report. Here is what he found in one street, Shelton Street.

▶ **SOURCE 9** *An artist's reconstruction of Shelton Street*

No. 26 The third floor. A man and a woman about 26 years old, who earned their living by making toys in the form of mice, which run round a wooden plate by the manipulation of a wire beneath. He making, and she selling. The room was fairly clean. No bedstead but a bundle rolled in the corner to sleep upon. One chair and a broken table at which they work and eat. In this way these people lived year after year.

No. 24 In the parlour to the left, a man (a labourer), a wife and two children. She strong, and clean in person. Both drank at times.

To the right lived Mrs O'Brien and her two boys. The husband is in hospital, leaving his wife in great poverty. Nothing in the house but a market basket, reversed to serve as a table at which the children would kneel, and a bundle of something in the corner to serve as a bed.

On the first floor the man is a sweep who lived with and abused a woman to death. He so knocked her about she was never free from bruises. His sons by another woman, as soon as they grew up, did the same and her own child died. The man spent all his pay on drink. Some weeks ago she came back from hospital, her head bound up, her arms black and blue. A few weeks later she was on her bed unconscious, with blackened eyes and face all bruised. She is now dead. There was no prosecution.

No. 20 In one of the parlours lived Burton and his wife. He was 60 years of age and was a scavenger. They had not a chair to sit on, and the room was swarming with vermin.

No. 4 In the ground floor room lived Mr and Mrs Shane and their four children. The eldest was fourteen. Mr Shane took cold from exposure and was groaning in bed for nine months before he finally died. Mrs Shane earns a living by selling watercress. This family was tidier than some, but the woman was given to drink at times. An older son was in prison.

On the first floor was a family of six, costermongers. They hire their barrows and buy early in the morning at Covent Garden, bring home what they buy, sort it over and then go out to sell it.

General notes

These houses contain cellars, parlours, and first, second and third floors, mostly two rooms on a floor. Few of the families who live here occupy more than one room.

The stairs at the end of the passage turn down as well as up. The kitchen parlour (like the first floor room) occupies the whole width of the house. There is usually a back kitchen with a wash house and scullery. The people who own the house usually only use the kitchens and let out the other floors.

The little yard at the back is just large enough for a dustbin and closet and water tap – all serving six or seven families. The water is drawn from a cistern that is always full of rubbish, sometimes a dead cat.

No. 28 On the second floor lived a widow with a son and two daughters. The widow sold flowers and watercress and had a stand at the West End, where she obtained coal, bread and soup tickets from sympathetic ladies. In her room lived her grown-up son, two daughters, and two or three children of one of these daughters.

Above on the third floor lived a market porter, his wife and four children. The cupboard often bare, the grate fireless, and the children without shoes or stockings, sometimes almost naked.

No. 4 On the second floor there was a woman with four small children, whose husband had gone to America. The children were without boots or food, and their mother had to lock them in the room while she went to sell oranges in the street.

On the third floor in two small rooms lived a family with two children. The man was paralysed and helpless. The son worked in a bakery and kept the family. The daughter had a child which died. The rooms of this family were filthy, and the family lived like pigs. Both sights and smells were sickening.

▼ **ACTIVITY**

It is 1881. You have been appointed as a researcher on the CENSUS for that year. You must report on the people living in Shelton Street. You have rough notes on each household as in Source 9.

1 Your teacher will give you a census form to complete for this street. It has the following headings: Address and floor; Name; Gender; Age; Married/Single; Occupation. Some of the information is not available (e.g. some names and ages) so you will have to leave those columns blank.

2 There are a number of references to deaths. Your teacher will give you another form to complete, with as much detail as you can, for each death. It has the following headings: Address and floor; Name; Gender; Age at death; Cause of death.

3 Now that you have organised all this information, write a report about the people in this street under the following headings: Occupations, Standard of living, Health and hygiene, and Size of families.

4 Choose any two of the people in Source 9. Write five questions you would want to ask them to find out more about their lives. What are the most important things you want to know?

Review: Was there more to a Victorian town than 'foul facts'?

▼ **DISCUSS**

Look back at your 'Ten foul facts on vile Victorian towns' (see page 62). Do you still think that they are a fair reflection of Victorian towns?

▼ **REVIEW ACTIVITY**

The great French historian Lucien Febvre wrote, 'A mere collector of facts is as useful as a collector of match-boxes.'

Your facts on the Victorian towns and cities are interesting but what is really important is the key question 'Is there more to a Victorian town than this?'

A historian must try to find the answer. This is how you will do it. You are going to produce a display panel (A3 size). At the centre you can put your 'foul facts'. Then all around it, or above and below it, write

BEYOND THE FOUL FACTS . . .

and write paragraphs or lists of bullet points on each of the following:

- transport
- work
- opportunity
- entertainment.

Finally, write a paragraph which sums up your answer to the question 'Why did people choose to live in towns if they were so horrible?'

DEPTH STUDY 4

THE VOTE

The wettest MP!
On the edge of England lies this borough of Dunwich. There are no people living here. The land was lost to the sea years ago. Yet the area sends an MP to Parliament!

You might think there is something wrong with a system that lets this happen. In the 1820s many people agreed. A few did not. In this depth study you will find out what Parliament did in 1832 to make voting fairer and why they did it. You will also find out why some people – called Chartists – were not at all satisfied and what they tried to do about it.

What was wrong with democracy in the 1820s?

▶▶ Britain prides itself on being a DEMOCRACY. But that meant something different in the 1820s from what it means today.

Your aim at the end of this enquiry will be to create your own political cartoon defending or criticising democracy in the 1820s.

Let's begin by finding out what the voting system was like in the 1820s.

Constituencies
- The country is divided into constituencies called counties and boroughs. Most send two MPs to Parliament.

Who can vote?

- Nobody under 21 can vote. No women at all are allowed to vote.
- In the counties only property owners can vote.
- In the boroughs the right to vote varies from place to place. In some boroughs, such as Westminster, nearly all the men can vote, in others very few can vote.

Who can be an MP?

- Only men can become MPs and they have to own a lot of property to be allowed to stand. MPs are not paid a salary so only rich people can afford to be MPs.

Parties
- Most MPs belong to one of the two main parties, the WHIGS and the TORIES.

How does voting take place?

- In many constituencies there is no contest. The local landowner is so influential (for example, because the voters work for him or are his tenants) that he is able to control the elections, and so no one bothers to stand against his candidates. (These were called 'pocket boroughs'. Gatton in Surrey was the worst example. It consisted of only six houses and the owner of these cottages controlled the election of two MPs.)
- In constituencies where there is a contest, threats and bribery are often used on the voters.
- Voting is not secret. In fact, voters have to announce for whom they are voting.

- The candidate who gets the most votes becomes an MP in the House of Commons.

When is there an election?
- There has to be a General Election at least every seven years. 7 YEARS

What do MPs do?
- MPs join the House of Commons where they make decisions about how the country should be run. However, the House of Lords is more important than the House of Commons.
  The Prime Minister usually comes from the House of Lords.

Rotten boroughs

These were boroughs with small numbers of voters who could be bribed. An extreme example is Dunwich in Suffolk. It had been destroyed by coastal erosion but 30 people who used to live there still had the right to elect two MPs. They sold their vote to the highest bidder.

Rural bias

Big cities like Manchester had no MPs, while some tiny villages sent two MPs to Parliament.

Southern bias

Southern counties had lots of MPs because they were full of ancient boroughs, e.g. Cornwall had 20 boroughs represented by 40 MPs in 1830. Northern counties where most people lived had very few MPs.

English bias

Scotland (49 MPs), Wales (27 MPs) and Ireland (97 MPs) were all under represented.

▼ DISCUSS

What do you think was most unfair about the system in the 1820s? Give your reasons.

▼ ACTIVITY

Copy the following table and use it to compare democracy in 1820 with democracy today.

1. Use the information on these pages to fill out column 2.
2. Use your own research to fill out column 3. If you need more information about today, your teacher will give you a sheet.
3. As a class, draw up a list of weaknesses of the voting system in the 1820s.

	1820	Today
Constituencies		
Who can vote?		
Who can be an MP?		
Parties		
How does voting take place?		
When is there an election?		
What do MPs do?		

Should we reform the system? No!

MP

> **Don't change the system if it is working!**
> Our electoral system has made Britain the richest and most powerful country in the world, and everybody has benefited from this.

Landowner

> **It's right that landowners have most influence!**
> Only landowners can be trusted to run the country well. Britain's wealth comes from the land. It is the land which feeds everyone. To have a say in the running of the country you should have a stake in it – you should own some land. Our families have been involved in running the country for generations. We have been born and educated to rule. People who have no permanent stake in the country might not be so bothered about how well the country is governed.

Rich Tory aristocrat

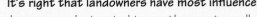

> **Reform leads to revolution!**
> Look at what happened in France when they tried to give more people a say in government. It ended in chaos! The King and Queen and all the best people were guillotined. The same could happen here. There have already been riots in Derby, Nottingham and Merthyr Tydfil. In Bristol 16 people were killed in the riots. Once the first reform has been passed others will follow! Democracy will mean the rule of the mob and the destruction of property.

Should we reform the system? Yes!

Industrialist

The House of Commons is full of landowners. They know nothing about industry. We need industrialists as MPs so that Britain's industrial future can be planned properly.
We do not want a revolution. All we want is to give more of the middle classes the vote and to let some of the prosperous middle classes into Parliament as MPs.

Newspaper editor

It is time to make some changes. Over the last 100 years Britain has been transformed. Britain's wealth now comes from industry and trade, not from farming. Yet large towns like Leeds, Manchester and Liverpool, with hundreds of thousands of people, do not have their own MPs. 'Rotten boroughs' like Dunwich have two MPs! Let's take those seats and give them to the towns with large populations.

Working-class radical: 1825

The ordinary people are suffering yet again! Because of the bad harvests and the slump in trade many ordinary people are out of work and starving. If they are in work their wages have been cut. Who is looking after us?
No one. Certainly not the government, which only looks after the rich landowners. We are not revolutionaries but we do want change. We must be given the vote so that we can elect a government which will pass reforms to help us to live decent lives.

Whig aristocrat

There is a real danger of revolution here, just as happened in France forty years ago. We must head this off by making changes now. If we give the vote to the middle classes then they will stand with us, not attack us.

▼ ROLE PLAY

1 Look back at your criticisms of the system in the 1820s from page 87. Did you come up with the same points as these speakers? If you had other ideas write a speech bubble to add to this page.
2 Work in pairs. Choose one character from page 88, and one from this page, and role play a discussion between them.
3 Swap roles and repeat the role play.

▼ DISCUSS

4 Which argument did you find easiest to role play?

Cartoon history

In the early 1800s political cartoons were very popular. Sources 1 and 2 are good examples. Now that you know something about the arguments for and against reform, see if you can work out what these two political cartoons are saying and how they are saying it.

▼ DISCUSS

1 Explain which cartoon is for reform and which is against it.
2 Look carefully at the labelled symbols or features in each cartoon. Choose one feature in each cartoon which you think is really important in getting the message across. So important that if you took it away it would be a much weaker cartoon. Explain your choice. See if others agree with you.
3 Choose one feature which you could get rid of and the cartoon would stay just as strong. Again explain your choice.
4 Which do you think is the most effective cartoon? Explain why.

▼ **SOURCE 1** *A cartoon from 1819 commenting on Parliamentary reform*

Radical Reform carrying a pike and wearing a Cap of Liberty, two symbols of the French Revolution

Ugly face covered by a mask

Defending herself with the sword of 'The Laws'

Lion of loyalty rushing to her rescue

Hidden under his cloak are such evils as Murder, Robbery and Starvation

Britannia representing Britain under attack. Her belt has the saying *Dieu et mon droit* (God and my right)

Supported by the rock of Religion

▼ **SOURCE 2** *A cartoon published in 1832 entitled* Old Sarum

The sun is rising on a new age

Constitution Hill in background shows welcome to Scots, etc.

Tree represents system of rotten boroughs

The names of these rotten boroughs are written on the nests in the tree

The birds sitting in the nests are the MPs

Names of leading Whig reformers like Earl Grey and Lord Lansdown on axes

Reformers on the left

Opponents of reform on the right

> You take our house when you do take the prop
> That doth sustain our house – you take our lives
> When you do take the means whereby we live.

▼ **ACTIVITY**

Now draw or design your own cartoon to put forward one side of the argument, you choose which. Remember what you learned from the discussion of Sources 1 and 2. Don't be too ambitious. Limit yourself to just a few symbols – so the reader can focus on the important points. Your teacher can give you an 'ideas' sheet if you need one.

Were the Chartists revolutionaries?

▶▶ **In 1832 the Reformers won. The Government passed what became known as the Great Reform Act. But a lot of people were disappointed by it. The let-down of the Great Reform Act led to another protest movement that was even more worrying to the Government: Chartism. On pages 92–97 you will consider whether the Chartists were really as revolutionary as the government seemed to think they were.**

The 1832 Reform Act was a disappointment to the working classes. They had taken part in demonstrations for reform, but they did not benefit from the Reform Act.

Working-class radicals: 1836

You don't need to wonder about my reaction to the 'Great' Reform Act, I'll tell you. The government has given in to the middle classes and ignored us. Bury has been given an MP but who is allowed to vote? Not us! In a town of over 15,000 people how many people get the vote? Only 459! We didn't riot but if we are ignored we might next time.

In 1836 London artisans formed the London Working Men's Association, which was led by William Lovett. They drew up a petition, or Charter, including the six demands shown in Source 1.

Over a million and a quarter people signed the 1836 petition, but when it was presented to Parliament in 1839 the MPs ignored it.

▶ **SOURCE 2** *The Chartists taking their petition to Parliament*

▼ ACTIVITY A

On a scale of 1–10, where 1 is 'not at all' and 10 is 'extremely', decide whether each of the demands of Source 1 sound revolutionary.

▼ **SOURCE 1** *A handbill handed out in the streets around Britain in 1836*

The Six Points
OF THE
PEOPLE'S CHARTER

1. **A VOTE** for every man twenty-one years of age, of sound mind, and not undergoing punishment for crime.
2. **SECRET BALLOT.**—To protect the elector in the exercise of his vote.
3. **NO PROPERTY QUALIFICATION** for Members of Parliament—this enabling the constituencies to return the man of their choice, be he rich or poor.
4. **PAYMENT OF MEMBERS,** thus enabling an honest tradesman, working man, or other person to serve a constituency, when taken from his business to attend to the interests of the country.
5. **EQUAL CONSTITUENCIES,** securing the same amount of representation for the same number of electors, instead of allowing small constituencies to swamp the vote of large ones.
6. **ANNUAL PARLIAMENTS,** thus presenting the most effectual check to bribery and intimidation, since though a constituency might be bought once in seven years (even with the ballot), no purse could buy a constituency (under a system of universal suffrage) in each ensuing twelve month; and since members, when elected for a year only, would not be able to defy and betray their constituents as now.

Why did so many people support Chartism?

Chartism was a mass movement. Tens of thousands came to their meetings. Hundreds of thousands called themselves 'Chartists'. Millions signed their petitions.

Chartism's official aim was to get the vote for working men. That was the big idea. But many people signed the petitions because they thought that big idea was the answer to a much more specific set of everyday problems. If working people had the vote then they could genuinely do something about their other grievances. Some of the things they also wanted are shown below.

▼ **SOURCE 3** *Chartist leader Joseph Stevens speaking in 1838*

If any man is asked why he wanted the vote he would answer so he could shelter himself and his family, have a good dinner on the table, and have as much wages as would keep him in plenty.

▼ **ACTIVITY B**

Again on a scale of 1–10, say whether you think each of the aims below is revolutionary.

Get rid of the workhouses

This new Poor Law is unjust. An unemployed man should not be sent to the workhouse when times are hard. He should be given food at home like in the old days.

Improve our living conditions

When cholera came in 1832 it killed thousands of us. That will happen again unless someone cleans up our towns.

Increase our wages

Factory owners don't pay us enough to live on. They must be forced to pay a decent wage.

Use men not machines

Machines and factories put men out of work. Someone must control the spread of machines or we'll all be unemployed.

The Newport Rising

After the government rejected the People's Charter there were violent disturbances in many parts of the country. Some of the most serious were in South Wales. There were riots and some Chartist leaders were imprisoned.

On the night of 3 November 1839 John Frost led several thousand miners and ironworkers in a march on Newport in South Wales. They were demanding the release of a popular Chartist leader, Henry Vincent. Some estimates suggest that as many as 30,000 men and a few women were involved, but they did not all go into Newport. Many waited in the surrounding villages. When Frost and his followers arrived in Newport on the morning of 4 November they found a force of special constables and 32 soldiers of the 45th Regiment in the town waiting for them. Sources 4–6 tell you what happened next.

▼ **SOURCE 4** *From the evidence of Edward Patton, a carpenter, during the trial of John Frost, the Chartists' leader, at Newport*

▼ **SOURCE 5** *Written by R.G. Gammage in his History of the Chartist Movement, 1854. Gammage was a Chartist, but he was opposed to the use of violent methods*

A company of soldiers was stationed at the Westgate Hotel. The crowd marched there, loudly cheering. The police fled into the hotel for safety. The soldiers were stationed at the windows, through which some of the crowd fired. The soldiers returned the fire. In about twenty minutes ten of the Chartists were killed on the spot, and 50 others wounded.

I saw 200 or 300 people armed with sticks with iron points. I did not see many guns. I never saw anything done to the windows of the Westgate Inn. I did not hear a crash of windows. They drew up in front of the Westgate. They asked for the prisoners. They came close to the door. Then a rush was made. Then I heard firing, and took to my heels. I was 25 yards from the Westgate when I heard a very loud voice say, 'No, never.' I could not say when the firing began. It is likely enough the firing began from the Westgate Inn.

Over the next few days thousands of soldiers were brought in to Newport. The Chartists returned to their homes and some leaders escaped abroad. However, despite the thousands involved, the authorities found it very difficult to identify and arrest many men, which was evidence of the strong solidarity in South Wales. In the end 90 Chartists were arrested.

A

Eight Chartists were sentenced to death but this was reduced to TRANSPORTATION for life to Australia. Most of the rest were found guilty and sentenced to imprisonment.

The Chartists showed great discipline. Despite the large numbers of people involved there were hardly any reports of looting, vandalism or random violence.

However, in the government's eyes the Rising simply confirmed that Chartism was a violent movement bent on revolution. In the government clampdown that followed, 500 Chartists were imprisoned, including their leaders William Lovett and Feargus O'Connor.

▲▼ **SOURCES 6A AND 6B** *Two contemporary engravings of events at Newport. They were used in newspapers and broadsheets*

B

▼ **DISCUSS**

1 **According to Sources 4 and 5 who was to blame for the violence?**
2 **In Sources 6A and 6B where are**
   a) **the Chartists**
   b) **the government troops?**
3 **What impression do these pictures give you of the Chartists?**
4 **Do Sources 4 and 5 agree or disagree with the pictures in Sources 6A and 6B?**
5 **What reasons can you think of for the different viewpoints?**

▼ **ACTIVITY**

6 **Complete this word bubble to give the government's version of events as expressed in Source 6B.**

> I was a soldier on duty in Newport on 4 November . . .

7 **Using the same scale of 1–10 that you used earlier, do you think the methods used by the Chartists at Newport sound revolutionary?**

Snapshots from the Chartist archive

The Newport Rising greatly worried the government. Ever since the French Revolution, when there was a riot MPs asked 'Is this the beginning of a revolution?' After Newport, whenever the Chartists were planning something the government sent troops to keep control. This makes the Chartists sound like revolutionaries. But were they?

The evidence available to the government must have been very confusing because many different things were done in the name of Chartism. Just as Chartists had a range of motives they also used **a range of methods.**

Here is a selection of sources from the Chartist archive.

▲ **SOURCE 7**   *The Stockport riots. In August 1842 Chartists joined a riot which broke open the workhouse in Stockport and handed out bread stored there to poor people*

▼ **SOURCE 9**   *Chartist leader Feargus O' Connor set up a company into which workers who had lost their jobs paid a small amount each week.   It purchased five estates where each worker was given some land to earn a living. These estates were called 'O' Connervilles'*

▲ **SOURCE 8**   *The 1842 petition. Feargus O' Connor organised a second petition demanding the right to vote. It was signed by 3 million people. Thousands of Chartists marched to Parliament to hand it over*

▲ **SOURCE 10**   *The Plug Plot. In 1842 there was a depression in the manufacturing industry. Workers were either laid off, put on short hours, or wages were reduced. Some Chartists helped organise strikes all over northern England and the Midlands. Where workers refused to strike, they broke in and removed the plug of the steam engines, so closing the factory down*

Postscript: the end of Chartism

In 1848 O'Connor tried one more Chartist petition. This time Chartists collected 6 million signatures. He planned a mass meeting for half a million people followed by a mass march to Parliament. It would be the biggest petition, the biggest meeting, the biggest march ever.

The reality was very different. Only 20,000 people turned up to the meeting – there were more troops than protesters. Only O'Connor was allowed to march to Parliament with the petition. When the petition was inspected it had 1.9 million signatures, not 6 million, and some of them were forged – including the Duke of Wellington, who had signed at least nine times! The meeting and the petition were seen as a fiasco. Chartism was finished as a mass movement. It would be another 50 years before most of the changes asked for were made.

However Chartist energy had not run out. Chartists instead devoted themselves to other causes.

▲ **SOURCE 11** *A* Punch *cartoon from 1848 of a hoax petition which included the signatures of Queen Victoria and the Duke of Wellington*

▼ ACTIVITY A

1 On the same scale of 1–10 explain whether you think each of the Chartist activities shown in the sources on page 96 were revolutionary.

2 Here are the measures the government used to deal with these Chartist activities:
   a) ignore it
   b) send in the troops, arrest, imprison or transport the organisers
   c) organise a House of Commons committee and announce that the activity is illegal and must be ended.

   Match each of these reactions to one of the actions featured in the sources. Beware – some of the reactions might fit more than one action.

▼ ACTIVITY B

You are now going to look back over your work on the Chartists to answer the key question: 'Were the Chartists revolutionaries?'

Copy and complete a table like this to help you record your ideas.

For column three it will help you to look back to how you rated the Chartists on the scale of 1–10.

Now use your table to help you write a six-minute radio programme on the subject of 'Were the Chartists revolutionaries?'

Question	Your notes	Does this suggest they were revolutionaries?
What were the Chartists' aims?		
What were the Chartists' methods?		
How did the government react?		
What did the Chartists achieve?		

Review: Did anything really change?

You have met this woman twice before. Now it is 1850. How would she answer the question 'What did Chartism achieve?'

Working-class radical: 1850

It sounds like we failed, doesn't it! And true, we didn't get the vote but we did make the government listen. We got a Ten Hour Act to limit working hours. This protects us against the worst mill owners. And we got a Public Health Act to encourage towns to improve our living conditions and make our towns healthier. But at what cost! My husband's health never recovered from his spell in prison. He died before he could see these changes happen. We won't give up, though. When we finally get the vote, and mark my words we will, then our children and others like them will be educated enough to use it wisely. I hope I live to see the day.

▼ REVIEW ACTIVITY

1 **Look back to the landowner featured on page 88. How would this defender of the old system react to the events of the 1830s and 1840s? Write three more speech bubbles for this man:**
   a) **for 1832 explaining his reaction to the Great Reform Act**
   b) **for 1839 explaining his reaction to the rising at Newport**
   c) **for 1848 explaining his reaction to the collapse of Chartism.**
   What do you think he would say about the developments at each stage?

2 **Now write a paragraph to give your own balanced answer to the question: 'Did the efforts of the reformers and the Chartists change anything?'**

DEPTH STUDY 5

VICTORIAN VALUES

The hardest workers!
It's not immediately obvious but this picture has heroes and villains. Who do you think are the artist's heroes? Who do you think are his villains? Why?

The artist called this painting *Work*! It was his celebration of hard work. Hard work was good. To the Victorians, hard work made you healthy and wealthy and it improved your morals, too. In this depth study you will find out about the things that the Victorians approved of and a few things that they did not.

What did the Victorians believe?

▶▶ **Do you think you can get inside someone else's mind? It's hard, but if you are serious about history it's worth trying. The next six pages are going to help you try. See if you can get inside the mind of Mr Oaks.**

▼ ACTIVITY

> I'm your guide round some Victorian source material. My name is Mr Oaks. I live a respectable life with my wife and two very well-behaved daughters. I work in the City of London and I live in the suburbs in a comfortable house.
>
> I am going to show you sources which tell you about my values – what I think is important in life.

These are some of the things which Mr Oaks values:

- **HARD WORK AND SELF-HELP** (getting richer or more clever through my own efforts)
- **FAMILY LIFE**
- **OBEDIENCE AND RESPECT** (for authority or parents)
- **KNOWING YOUR PLACE IN SOCIETY** (and being content with it)
- **DIFFERENT ROLES FOR MEN AND WOMEN**
- **MODESTY** (not showing off) **AND DECENCY**
- **CHARITY** (helping others less fortunate than yourself)
- **RELIGION** (believing in God and helping others to do so as well).
- **TECHNOLOGY**
- **THE BRITISH EMPIRE**

1 Write each value heading on a card like this:

VALUE: Hard work and self-help

The Victorians believed that ...

2 As you study each source on pages 100–105:
a) Decide which value the source relates to. Speech bubbles from Mr Oaks like this will guide you.

> This source will help you with your ... card.

However some sources could help you with more than one value.

b) Next, write notes on the cards to explain in your own words what Victorians believed. For example, the card below could be written for Source 1:

VALUE: Obedience and respect

The Victorians believed that ...
it was important for children to respect their parents. God would punish anyone who did not respect their parents.

▼ SOURCE 1 *A poem from a Victorian book called* Divine and Moral Songs for Children

Have you not heard what dreadful plagues,
Are threatened by the Lord,
To him who breaks his father's laws,
Or mocks his mother's word?

What heavy guilt upon him lies!
How cursed is his name!
The ravens shall pick out his eyes
And eagles eat the same.

> This tells you about respect for parents. Make notes about it on your 'Obedience and respect' card.

3 Remember to keep these cards, because you are going to use them for a debate later on.

There's no doubt in my mind that this man should put his family first. Fill out a 'Family life' card.

◄ **SOURCE 2**
An engraving called Myself? Or the children? It shows a working man, and was published in 1872 to illustrate a Christmas story

I admire this boy's dedication. Fill out a 'Hard work and self-help' card

I also like what the girl is doing. Write out a 'Different roles for men and women' card.

◄ **SOURCE 3**
Kit's Writing Lesson, *painted in 1852 by R.B. Martineau. Boys who wanted office jobs had to practise their handwriting until it was perfect*

This picture shows you an image of an ideal family. Add a description of this ideal family to your 'Family life' card.

▲ **SOURCE 4** A painting by William Powell Frith called Many Happy Returns of the Day. *It shows an ideal Victorian family in a middle-class home in 1880*

▼ **SOURCE 5** *From an article written by G.H. Law in 1831*

The Almighty has given to his creatures different abilities and strengths, both of mind and body. There must be the Thinker, the Politician, the Craftsman, and . . . at the same time, the hewers of wood and the drawers of water. On the combined operation of all . . . depends the proper working, and the harmony, of the great machine of the world.

This is a difficult idea, but very important. Write a 'Knowing your place in society' card.

▼ **SOURCE 6** *Written by Dr Hodgson, whose views on education were widely respected in the nineteenth century*

There is a strong male instinct that a learned or even over-accomplished woman is one of the most intolerable monsters in creation.

This is a little harsh but there's a germ of truth in it. Add this to your 'Different roles for men and women' card.

CROMER URBAN DISTRICT.

BYE-LAWS
AS TO
PUBLIC BATHING

The following are the appointed Stands for Bathing Machines.

No. of Stand.	Description or limits of Stand.	Sex to which appropriated.
1	Between the Doctor's Steps Groyne and the Cart Gangway - - - -	FEMALE
2	Between the Doctor's Steps Groyne and a point 100 yards to the East thereof— Before the hour of 8 a.m. daily - - After the hour of 8 a.m. daily - -	 MALE MALE & FEMALE
3	To the East of a point 200 yards to the East of the Doctor's Steps Groyne, being 100 yards East of the Easternmost limit of Stand No. 2 - - - -	 MALE
4	To the West of Melbourne House Groyne— Before the hour of 8 a.m. daily - - After the hour of 8 a.m. daily - -	 MALE MALE & FEMALE

GENTLEMEN bathing in the Mixed Bathing Ground must wear a suitable costume, from neck to knee.

Copies of the Bye-laws may be obtained at the Offices of the Council. Persons offending against the Bye-laws are liable to a Penalty of £5.

By Order,

P. E. HANSELL,

Cromer, April, 1898. *Clerk to the District Council.*

◄ **SOURCE 7** *Laws about bathing at the seaside resort of Cromer in 1898*

> This will help you fill out a 'Modesty and decency' card.

▼ **SOURCE 9** *Adapted from a best-selling book called Self-help, written by Samuel Smiles in 1859*

Self-help is the root of all genuine growth in the individual. Whatever is done *for* people takes away the need of doing it for themselves . . . The best that institutions can do is to leave man free to improve himself. No laws can make the idle work, the spendthrift save, or the drunk sober.

> My favourite book, from my favourite writer and publisher! Add notes to your 'Hard work and self-help' card.

▼ **SOURCE 10** *Written by a school inspector in the 1870s*

The habit of obedience to authority . . . may tend to teach the working classes a lesson which many so sadly need in the North of England . . .
Submission to authority, deference to others . . . those are the real marks of manly self-respect and independence.

> Very important, this. Add it to your 'Obedience and respect' card.

▼ **SOURCE 8** *A report of the activities of Carr's Lane Chapel in Birmingham in 1859*

We now raise nearly £500 per year. For the Colonial Missionary Society we raise £70. For our Sunday and day schools (with nearly 200 children), we raise £200. We support two town missionaries at a cost of £200.
Our ladies also help in orphan mission schools. They work for the poor of the town. We also have night schools for young men and women, and Bible classes.

> This source will help you with your 'Charity' card.

You've already studied this source, so I'll leave you on your own with this one.

◀ **SOURCE 11** *A plate made in 1887 to celebrate the 50th anniversary of Queen Victoria's coronation*

Think hard about this. We all need to be reminded of our duty to others and to the poor. As a wealthy man I have responsibilities. This pricks my conscience. Add notes to your 'Charity' card.

▼ **SOURCE 12** *A cartoon about 'sweated labour' by George Cruikshank, published in the 1840s*

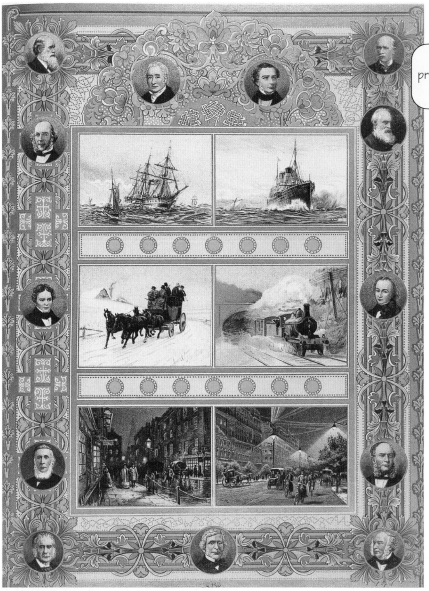

Write a 'Technology' card about being proud of British achievements – fast trains; fast ships; and great inventors.

◄ **SOURCE 13** *From the Illustrated London News, 1897. It shows changes during the 60 years of Queen Victoria's reign. Around the outside are great British scientists, engineers and inventors*

Sources 14 and 15 should give you more for your 'British Empire' card.

▼ **SOURCE 14** *Adapted from an article by Joseph Chamberlain, Britain's Colonial Secretary, in* Scribner's Magazine, *1898*

In countries where the great majority of the population are natives, the only sure way to develop the resources of the country is to provide the native population with white superintendents, and with rulers and administrators who will bring the knowledge they have derived from their experience in a higher civilisation to their task of running that country . . . who will always be led by the standards and ideals which they have been brought up to respect. This is the root idea of British dominion in the tropics.

▼ **SOURCE 15** *From a guide to the London and Birmingham and Grand Junction Railway, 1839*

It is a proud feeling to an Englishman to know that the products of the thousand busy hands and whirling wheels around him are destined to increase the comfort, refinement or splendour of nations spread far and wide over the globe.

Mr Oaks is now going to leave you for a few pages. But keep your cards and keep him in mind as you read pages 106–109. You will still be thinking about his attitudes.

How did the Victorians try to help the poor?

►► During the nineteenth century upper-class and middle-class people slowly became more aware of the conditions in which the poor lived and worked. Most people thought that the poor should be helped. But they couldn't agree on how to do it. On pages 106–109 you will investigate different ways in which help was given.

▼ **ACTIVITY A**

Look at your Victorian value cards.
1 Use Source 1 to add to your 'Modesty and decency' card.
2 Use Source 2 to add to your 'Hard work and self-help' card.

The Poor Law

The Poor Law was the way the government helped the poor. Before the Victorian period, the Poor Law said that each parish had to look after its own poor. Those who could not work (the old, mothers, the handicapped) were given small sums of money. Children were often trained in a local trade. Poor people who were fit to work were also given POOR RELIEF.

By 1830 about £7 million a year was being spent on the poor. This had to be paid for by the property owners in each town, through their local tax called 'rates'. Many rate-payers complained that they were paying people to be lazy and to avoid work. In 1834 the Poor Law Amendment Act was passed by Parliament. OUTDOOR RELIEF was abolished, and instead the poor would now all be put into workhouses.

The workhouse

The conditions in the workhouses were intended to be so grim that only those genuinely in need of help would apply to enter.

▼ **SOURCE 1** *Government regulations for workhouses, 1835*

1 The pauper [poor person] shall be thoroughly cleansed and shall be clothed in a workhouse dress.
2 Every pauper shall be searched and all articles taken from him.
3 The paupers shall be classed as follows:

- sick men
- able-bodied males aged fifteen and over
- boys aged seven to fifteen
- sick women
- able-bodied females aged fifteen and over
- girls aged seven to fifteen
- children under seven.

Each class shall be assigned to a separate building. Each class shall not communicate with those of another class.
The master shall allow the father or mother of any child in that same workhouse to have an interview with that child.

▼ **SOURCE 2** *Written in the nineteenth century by John Beecher*

The inferior classes must be forced to see how demoralising and degrading poor relief is and how sweet and wholesome is that independence which is earned by perseverance and honest hard work.

▼ **SOURCE 3** *Workhouse regulations, 1835*

The following offences are to be punished:

- making a noise when silence is ordered
- using obscene language
- refusing to work
- pretending to be sick
- climbing over the boundary wall of the workhouse.

No corporal punishment shall be inflicted on any female child.
No corporal punishment shall be inflicted on any male child, except with a rod approved of by the Guardians of the workhouse.

▼ SOURCE 4 *From the plans drawn by the Poor Law Commissioners to show what the new workhouses should be like*

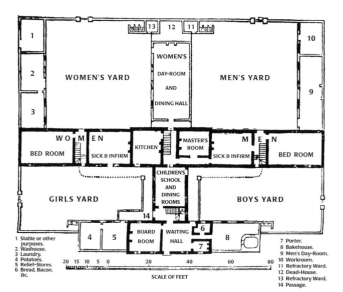

1 Stable or other purposes.
2 Washouse.
3 Laundry.
4 Potatoes.
5 Relief-Stores.
6 Bread, Bacon, &c.

7 Porter.
8 Bakehouse.
9 Men's Day-Room.
10 Workroom.
11 Refractory Ward.
12 Dead-House.
13 Refractory Ward.
14 Passage.

Breakfast
7oz of bread
$1\frac{1}{2}$ pints of gruel

Dinner
$1\frac{1}{2}$ pints of beef and vegetable soup

Supper
6oz of bread
2oz of cheese

▲ SOURCE 5 *The typical workhouse diet*

▼ SOURCE 6 *An illustration for Charles Dickens' novel* Oliver Twist, *1837. Oliver is in the workhouse. He is asking for more food, but the workhouse master refuses. The inmates were allowed a certain amount of food and no more*

▼ SOURCE 7 The daily routine for children in the workhouse			
	8a.m.	**1p.m.**	**2.30p.m.**
Girls	Learning to read and write	Dinner	Knitting and sewing
Boys	Work in the card room	Dinner	Reading and writing in the schoolroom

▼ ACTIVITY B

The Victorians wanted to make life in the workhouse hard and demoralising for the paupers.

1 *How* did they do this? Make a list of all the methods they used, using Sources 1–7 to help you.

2 *Why* did they do this? Look at Source 2 for some clues.

▼ DISCUSS

3 Do you think that we have a better or worse way of dealing with the poor today? Be ready to give reasons.

The strange story of Harriet Kettle

Harriet Kettle spent most of her early life in Victorian institutions. Because she caused a lot of trouble we know a lot about her early life! Almost everywhere she lived people made notes about her insolent or violent behaviour. Here is a brief outline of Harriet Kettle's life.

▼ **SOURCE 8** *From workhouse records, 28 April 1851*

Harriet Kettle was again brought before the Board charged with repeatedly disobeying the schoolmistress. She was ordered to be kept in a separate apartment for six hours a day for four days.

▼ **SOURCE 9** *From workhouse records, 7 January 1856*

Harriet Kettle violently refused to perform the work ordered by the Master because she was refused clothes to leave the workhouse.

▼ **SOURCE 10** *From Little Walsingham prison records, 11 July 1856*

The prisoners have been orderly and respectful, with the exception of Harriet Kettle, whose conduct has been most violent and disobedient and who has lately become a suicidal lunatic.

Kettle, Harriet. Admitted 16 July 1856. Her case is put down to a naturally bad temper and from her irregular life, she having been a prostitute in Norwich for some years before her committal to prison for having assaulted the master of a workhouse.

▼ SOURCE 12 *From the Norfolk Chronicle, 31 March 1860, reporting the trial of Harriet Kettle for arson*

The prisoner Harriet Kettle exhibited the utmost excitement, and acted as though she was insane. She declared she would take her own life and that no man should conquer her.

The prisoner was charged with attempting to set fire to the Mitford and Launditch Union House at Gressenhall on 20 November 1858.

The master of the workhouse stated that on the day named his attention was called to the prisoner's beating the assistant matron in the dining hall. He assisted in removing the prisoner, and put her into a separate apartment. She then declared that she would burn down the 'b—y building', and soon after he went into the room, and found some straw on the floor which had been ripped out of a bed in the room. The straw had just been set fire to. He put the fire out. She was subsequently taken before a magistrate.

The Master of Thorpe Lunatic Asylum said he did not think she was insane, but that she was subject to violent fits of passion, especially when thwarted.

The learned judge summed up, saying it was quite possible for the prisoner to behave in this violent manner for the purpose of escaping punishment.

The jury found her guilty. The prisoner was sentenced to eighteen months' hard labour.

▼ SOURCE 13 *From the records of the County Lunatic Asylum, 10 July 1863*

Harriet Kettle was admitted 10 July 1863. She was brought up in Gressenhall Workhouse, which she left while still quite a girl. From this point her evil courses date. Inheriting a bad attitude and violent passions, deprived of a mother's care, and being brought up surrounded by the moral filth of a workhouse, a place unfavourable to any improvement in character, it is not surprising that when set free in the world she got into trouble.

She is very short, and small, neat and tidy in her person, quick and intelligent. Her features are somewhat coarse, the lips thick, and her face has a repulsive look, showing cunning, low breeding.

She blames the world for some of her follies, and says she could not earn a living honestly, not being strong enough for service. She has had a cough for a long time, is thin and frequently spits blood.

▼ ACTIVITY

1839 Harriet was born in a Norfolk village, the daughter of a farm labourer.
1845 Her mother died insane. Her father rejected her.
1851 Harriet was living in the workhouse at Gressenhall.
1864 She was discharged from the Norfolk Lunatic Asylum.
1865 She married an agricultural labourer and over the next few years had four children.
1891 By now Harriet was a grandmother.

1 On your own copy of this timeline add the extra detail given in Sources 8–13.

▼ DISCUSS

2 Who does Source 13 blame for Harriet Kettle's problems?
3 Do you think Mr Oaks (see page 100) would agree or disagree with Source 13? Give reasons to support your answer.

Why did Annie Besant want to help poor people?

▶▶ **One way to help the poor was to help them help themselves. That was what Annie Besant tried to do, although others said she was a meddlesome troublemaker. See what you think.**

In 1888 a SOCIALIST called Annie Besant interviewed some women who worked at the Bryant and May factory in the East End of London. The factory produced matches and matchboxes. She was shocked by the working conditions and pay: the women could be hit or fined by the foreman, and some were paid only one penny per hour.

▲ **SOURCE 2** *Annie Besant (1847–1933)*

▼ **SOURCE 1** *A summary of conditions in the factory, as reported by Annie Besant*

- Ventilation in the factory has been destroyed by building an extra storey.
- Phosphorus fumes from the matches cause 'phossy jaw', a form of bone cancer. Phosphorus has been banned in the USA because it is so dangerous.
- Meal breaks are taken in the work area, so the women eat the phosphorus along with their food. This leads to loss of teeth and baldness.
- The work is winter work only. In the summer the women have to find other work if they can.
- Women are fined for talking, going to the toilet or dropping matches.
- The hours are 6.30 a.m. to 6.00 p.m. with only two short meal breaks.
- The pay is $2\frac{1}{4}$d for making 144 boxes. For making matches it is about $2\frac{1}{4}$d an hour. The women earn about four shillings a week.

Annie Besant published her findings in an article called *White Slavery in London*. As you would expect, Bryant and May were not very pleased. The women who had spoken to Besant were sacked, and the others were ordered to sign a document saying that conditions in the factory were good.

With Besant's help, however, the women formed a union and went on strike. Many newspapers and members of the public took the side of the match workers and within three weeks the company gave in. The fines were stopped and working conditions were improved.

Annie Besant moved to India in 1893 and became involved in movements for social and political reform, in particular the campaign for Indian Independence. The British ruler called her **'That terrible old lady who has given me infinite trouble'**.

▼ **SOURCE 3** *From an article in* The Times, *June 1888*

The pity is that the matchgirls have not taken their own course but have been egged on to strike by irresponsible advisers. No effort has been spared by these pests of the modern industrialised world to bring the quarrel to a head.

The matchgirls have expressed their determination to hold out and they stick together well. The arrangements for strike pay have been made with great thoroughness. Not one of them gets less than four shillings.

Certain people have the idea that this firm, so far from being of use to the locality, does much to oppress labourers. This is a baseless rumour.

The appearance of the factory and the people who work in it are each suggesting of hard work, good order and a fair day's wages being earned for a fair day's work. Our workers were thoroughly happy with us until the socialistic influence of outside agitators started to disturb their minds. I have no doubt that they have been influenced by the twaddle of Mrs Besant and other socialists.

▲ **SOURCE 4** *From a statement by Bryant and May in June 1888, during the strike*

◄ **SOURCE 5** *A contemporary drawing of the match workers put out by Bryant and May.*

▼ **SOURCE 6** *A photograph of the match factory in the 1890s*

▼ DISCUSS

1 Why might Mr Oaks (see page 100) have sided with Annie Besant?
2 Why might he have sided with Bryant and May?
3 Who do you think he would have had most sympathy with?
4 Compare Sources 5 and 6. Explain how they differ.
5 Which is more reliable for telling us what working conditions in the factory were really like?
6 How is the other source useful to a historian studying the strike?
7 Who does Source 3 blame for the strike?
8 Who do you think was to blame for the strike? Explain your answer.

Review: Victorian values

When looking back at the nineteenth century – and particularly at the Victorian era – people see different things.

Some people look back longingly. They see the grand buildings which the Victorians built. They respect the Victorians' pride in being British. They agree with the Victorians' idea that people should improve their own situation, rather than depend on the government. They admire the Victorians. When they use the word 'Victorian' they mean 'principled', 'strong', 'ambitious'.

Other people distrust the values of Victorian Britain. They argue that Victorian bosses exploited their workers. They dislike Victorian snobbishness. They criticise the way the Victorians were prejudiced against people from other countries or races. When they use the word 'Victorian' they mean 'old-fashioned' or 'intolerant' or 'uncaring'. Which side are you on?

The good old days

The bad old days

▼ REVIEW ACTIVITY

What do you think of Victorian values?

You are now going to use your value cards to help you prepare a speech for a debate on the motion:

VICTORIAN VALUES WERE GOOD VALUES!

You can argue for or against the motion. This is how to do it:

1 **Collect together all your cards. You can work in groups and pool your cards if you wish.**
2 **Decide whether you want to argue for or against the motion. It doesn't have to be what you personally think: it's quite a useful skill to be able to argue someone else's case for them.**
3 **Select all the cards which support your viewpoint that Victorian values were/were not good values.**
4 **Choose TWO only that you are going to use in your speech.**
5 **Give reasons and evidence from this book to support your view that this was/was not a good value.**
6 **Write your speech. You could start:**

I wish to argue for/against this motion. I think that Victorian values were _____

_____

I have two examples to support my case. The first is _____

_____

This is a good/not a good value because _____

_____

The second example is _____

_____

This is a good/not a good value because _____

_____

In conclusion, I think we should admire/be suspicious of Victorian values because _____

_____

112 ▲

Glossary

ABOLITION banning something, e.g. slavery

AMPUTATE removing a limb by surgery

ARTISAN a skilled manual worker

CASH CROPS crops such as cotton, grown not for food but to be sold

CENSUS an official count of the population of a country

CHARTIST(S) a member of the group demanding reform of the voting system between 1837 and 1848. Called after their People's Charter of six demands

CHOLERA a disease carried in water supplies contaminated by sewage. It is usually fatal

COLONY/IES a country ruled by another country

DEMOCRACY a system of government where the whole population has the right to vote for their government in regular elections

DEPOTS the place from where a company trades

DIVISION OF LABOUR the division of work into specialised tasks, each performed by a different person or group

DOMESTIC SYSTEM the main system of making goods before the Industrial Revolution. People worked in their own homes

DYSENTERY a disease of the intestines

ENTREPRENEUR someone who makes money from establishing a business

EXPORT transporting and selling goods that are made in Britain abroad

INDUSTRIAL REVOLUTION the time of great change when people began to make goods in factories using machines

IMPORT when goods are brought into Britain from abroad

INVEST pay money for the development of a project, for example to buy a factory or develop a new machine

MARKETS countries or areas of countries where traders sell their goods

MANUFACTURER A factory owner, or someone who produces goods

NAVVY/NAVVIES railway labourer/s

OVERSEER a person in charge of a group of workers

PATENT a document granting a person the sole right to make, use or sell a new invention

PAUPER APPRENTICES orphans who were sent to work in mills by the authorities who looked after them (usually in the large towns)

PLANTATIONS estates in the West Indies where sugar cane was grown or estates in the southern United States where cotton was grown

POOR RELIEF/OUTDOOR RELIEF money paid to poor people who continued to live in their own homes

QUAKER a type of Christian with a strong belief in peace

RAJA/RANI the title for male and female Indian rulers

RAW MATERIALS natural materials such as coal or cotton which have to be turned into finished goods in a factory

SHARES when a company wants to raise money it sells shares in the company. This entitles the people who buy them to a share in the profits

SLAVE someone owned by another person

SOCIALIST a person who believes that the community as a whole should own businesses rather than individuals

TORIES the political party in the eighteenth and nineteenth centuries which supported the existing political and religious system

TRANSPORTED sent as a punishment to live in another country (at this time people were sent to Australia)

WHIGS the political party in the eighteenth and nineteenth centuries which supported reform

WORKHOUSE a place where poor people were forced to live if they wanted to be given food, clothing and shelter

Index